Name ______________________

Rule The letters **k**, **ck**, or **que** usually stand for the /k/ sound.

EXAMPLES

Letters	Word	Sound
k	**k**ing	/k/
ck	ti**ck**le	/k/
que	opa**que**	/k/

Directions Read the following story. Circle each word that has the /k/ sound.

The Shaggy Bird

Imagine, if you will, a bird that does not fly and has a stocky body about the size of a chicken, with feathers that look like hair and no tail.

Is this a joke, you ask, or perhaps some kind of freakish dream?

Definitely not! The kiwi is a bird whose physique is unique. If you would like to visit this bird, seek it in the thick, wet forests of New Zealand. Keep your eyes open and look quickly, though. These birds are afraid of people.

Rule When the letters **qu** appear at the beginning of a word, they usually stand for the /kw/ sound .

EXAMPLES

queen	**qu**arter	**qu**ilt
quick	**qu**intet	**qu**iet

Directions Write a word from the box to complete each sentence.

question	quake	qualms	quarter	quick

1. Carla's legs began to ________________ as she heard, "On Your Mark!"
2. She had ________________ about entering this race.
3. Carla was as ________________ as a deer, but so was her rival Jenny.
4. Then Carla's coach said there was no ________________ that she was ready.
5. She fingered her lucky ________________ as the starter yelled, "Go!"

Rule The letters **ch** usually stand for the sound at the beginning and end of **church**. Sometimes **ch** can stand for the /k/ or /sh/ sounds.

EXAMPLES

Letters	Word	Sound
ch	**ch**icken	/ch/
ch	**ch**orus	/k/
ch	**ch**ivalry	/sh/

Directions Circle each word with **ch** in the sentences. Then write each circled word in the correct column below the sentences.

1. Charlotte's party went off right on schedule.
2. Charles led a small orchestra in playing "Happy Birthday."
3. The new student came in a chauffeur-driven car.
4. A special chef made chocolate cake.
5. Carrie brought some chopped chives and bean dip.
6. Our stomachs ached, but we played charades anyway.

/k/	/ch/	/sh/
______	______	______
______	______	______
______	______	______
______	______	______

Directions Circle each word in which **kn** stands for the /n/ sound.

Rule **Kn** stands for the /n/ sound in **knee**. The **k** is silent.

1. Sandy has always had a knack for camping.
2. He packs his knapsack carefully.
3. First he puts his scout knife into the flap.
4. Next he folds his knitted cap and gloves.
5. When everything is packed, he ties a secure knot.

Name ____________________

Rule When the letter **c** comes before **a**, **o**, or **u**, it usually stands for the /k/ sound. When **c** comes before **e**, **i**, or **y**, it usually stands for the /s/ sound.

Examples

Letters	Word	Sound
c	**c**oat	/k/
c	silen**c**e	/s/

Directions Underline each word in the sentences that contains a **c.** Then write /k/ or /s/ above each **c** word to show its sound.

1. For centuries, people have wanted to comprehend outer space.
2. Was it a cold place, or perhaps a region of fierce heat?
3. It has been over three decades since Sputnik's flight in 1957.
4. The U.S. space center is located at Cape Canaveral, Florida.
5. There, audiences anticipate the countdown as spacecraft are sent into space.
6. In the cabin, astronauts rely on computers to control the blastoff.
7. Often a spacecraft races into the cosmos without human company.
8. Perhaps it will circle a planet or film a streaking comet.
9. Maybe it will carry a communications satellite as cargo.
10. Humans seem to welcome the excitement of facing the unknown.

Rule The letters **g** and **dge** can stand for the /j/ sound as in **page** and **bridge**. Sometimes **g** stands for the hard /g/ sound as in **gate**.

EXAMPLES

Letters	Word	Sound
g	giggle	/g/
g	gem	/j/
dge	fu**dge**	/j/

Directions Read each word below. Write /g/ in the blank if the word has the hard **g** sound. Write /j/ if the word contains the **j** sound.

1. region ____	**2.** wedges ____	**3.** giant ____	**4.** ridge ____
5. stage ____	**6.** guest ____	**7.** gobbled ____	**8.** gym ____
9. gorillas ____	**10.** sponge ____	**11.** disgust ____	**12.** edge ____

Directions Write the word from the list above that completes each sentence.

1. We met on the ________________ to build the set for the play.

2. Our play is about saving the wild ________________.

3. First we had to make the stage look like a jungle ________________.

4. This is the area in which the ________________ apes live.

5. We soon stopped for lunch, but Harry had ________________ all the sandwiches.

6. "Act your age," snapped Marla in ________________.

7. Later, we had to pound ________________ under the sets to make them stand straight.

8. Finally we all sat on the ________________ of the stage and rested.

Name ____________________

Directions Read the words in the box. Then read the story. Write the correct word from the box to complete each unfinished sentence.

protective	goal	stocky	century	back
tackling	protect	because	block	physiques

Football and Safety

The team with the ball lines up to form a *T.* The quarterback drops ____________________ and gives the ball to the fullback. As his players ____________________ for him, the ____________________ fullback carries the football across the ____________________ line. Touchdown! The crowd goes wild.

Did you ever wonder how football began? Some people think the game got started in the middle of the last ____________________. Back then, there were no ____________________ uniforms or helmets. None were needed ____________________ the game was very similar to soccer.

Over the years, football players gradually increased the amount of running, blocking, and ____________________. To accomplish this, players had to have the strongest of ____________________. Even so, football players were often injured. Helmets, pads, and uniforms were developed to better ____________________ the players.

Directions Read each word. Write the letter of the paraphrase that has the same meaning. Then read the story and rewrite it, paraphrasing each word or word group in boldface print. Use the words in the list to help you.

Hint There are many different ways you can tell about the same facts. When a sentence or paragraph uses different words to tell about the facts, the sentences or paragraphs are paraphrases of the facts.

____	**1.**	unique	**a.**	one-of-a-kind
____	**2.**	clever	**b.**	strange
____	**3.**	became	**c.**	was
____	**4.**	gained	**d.**	once in a while
____	**5.**	occasionally	**e.**	invented
____	**6.**	conceived	**f.**	regularly
____	**7.**	peculiar	**g.**	won
____	**8.**	commonly	**h.**	smart

Chess Greats

Chess is a **one-of-a-kind** game. The idea for chess was probably **invented** in India about 1,500 years ago. Through the years, there have been some imaginative and **smart** players.

For example, in the early 1900s, Harry Nelson Pillsbury got into a **strange** habit. He **regularly** played 12 to 16 chess games at once—while blindfolded.

Once in a while people become skillful chess players at a very early age. Samuel Reshevsky **was** a chess master at age eight. Bobby Fischer **won** the U.S. chess title in 1958 at age fourteen.

Name ______________________________

Rule The letters **f**, **ff**, or **ph** usually stand for the /f/ sound.

EXAMPLES

Letters	Word	Sound
f	**f**ish	/f/
ff	ta**ff**y	/f/
ph	tele**ph**one	/f/

Definition An **analogy** compares different things. Analogies show how pairs of things are alike.

EXAMPLE

A **car** is to a **road** as a **boat** is to **water**.

A car travels over a road, and a boat travels over water.

Directions Circle the correct ending for each analogy. Then draw a box around the letter or letters that stand for the /f/ sound in each underlined word.

1. **Leaf** is to **tree** as **feather** is to
   cabin. snake. bird.
2. **Sea** is to **fishing** as **field** is to
   calling. farming. swimming.
3. **Last** is to **final** as **phony** is to
   fake. end. phone.
4. **Neck** is to **giraffe** as **trunk** is to
   robin. pack. elephant.
5. **Telephone** is to **talking** as **pamphlet** is to
   speaking. reading. phoning.
6. **Feet** is to **foot** as **fingers** is to
   toe. finger. fine.
7. **Phantom** is to **ghost** as **end** is to
   start. elf. finish.
8. **Camera** is to **photo** as **tape recorder** is to
   walls. picture. recording.
9. **Baker** is to **flour** as **florist** is to
   flowers. floors. glasses.
10. **Niece** is to **nephew** as **aunt** is to
    fly. uncle. lion.

Rule The letters **gh** can stand for the /g/ or /f/ sounds. Sometimes **gh** is silent and stands for no sound.

EXAMPLES

Letters	Word	Sound
gh	**gh**ost	/g/
gh	lau**gh**	/f/
gh	nau**gh**ty	no sound

Directions Read each sentence and underline the word or words with **gh.** Then write each **gh** word in the correct column at the bottom to show its sound.

1. I hoped we would have enough food for our community party.
2. I sighed as I realized I had practically bought out the grocery store.
3. I got bread and rolls, olives, and gherkin pickles.
4. I got extra-lean meat so it wouldn't be tough.
5. Some of the neighbors were making salads and desserts.
6. I thought about the ghastly party we had during a blizzard last year.
7. The snow-covered guests arrived looking like ghosts.
8. It seemed that everyone was coughing and sneezing.
9. The howling wind made a ghostly sound in the chimney.
10. Afterwards everyone laughed about it.

/f/	/g/	no sound
________	________	________
________	________	________
________	________	________
________	________	________

Name ____________________

Rule The consonant **s** usually stands for the sound you hear at the beginning of **silent**. Sometimes **s** can stand for /z/, /sh/, or /zh/.

EXAMPLES

Letter	Word	Sound
s	soccer	/s/
s	posy	/z/
s	sugar	/sh/
s	treasure	/zh/

Directions Write each word in the box on the line beside its definition. Then write /s/, /z/, /sh/, or /zh/ to show the sound that **s** stands for in that word.

noisy	miser	similar	tissue	harvest	insurance
reservoir	hasten	Russian	measure	leisure	research

1. leisure /zh/ free time
2. ________ ____ a place that holds an extra, or reserve, supply; often a lake where water is collected
3. ________ ____ careful, patient study of something
4. ________ ____ a light, thin cloth or paper
5. ________ ____ full of clamor or sounds
6. ________ ____ find the exact dimensions of something
7. ________ ____ almost, but not exactly, the same
8. ________ ____ a greedy or stingy person who hoards money
9. ________ ____ a policy or contract guaranteeing protection from loss
10. ________ ____ gathering of a crop
11. ________ ____ to speed up; to move or act swiftly
12. ________ ____ a native of the U.S.S.R.

Directions The sentences in the paragraphs below include words that contain **s**. The sentences are not in the correct sequence. Number each group of sentences in the correct order. Then underline each **s** that has the /s/ sound and circle each **s** that has the /z/ sound.

1.

____ However, her morose mood doesn't often last long.

____ Sometimes Sally Simpson feels sad.

____ Here is how it works: Sally puts a crimson plastic rose between her teeth and vigorously hums the song "Deck the Halls."

____ This is because Sally enjoys making others laugh.

2.

____ The combination of drums, saxophone, and horns was too much.

____ After two "For Sale" signs appeared overnight, my parents suggested that we play one of their favorite songs—"Far, Far Away."

____ I've always loved music, so one day I decided to compose some songs.

____ When I succeeded in writing several pieces, I invited my friends Sally, Susan, and Sam over to play them.

Directions Choose four of the **s** words from the sentences above and use them in original sentences of your own.

____

____

____

____

____

____

____

____

Name ______________________________

Rule The letters **wh** can stand for the /h/ sound as in **who** or for the /hw/ sound as in **what**.

EXAMPLES

Letters	Word	Sound
wh	**wh**ole	/h/
wh	**wh**irl	/hw/

Directions Use a word from the box to complete each sentence. Then write /h/ or /hw/ on the line at the right to show which sound the word contains.

where	wheelchair	what	wharf
whiff	whole	whistle	whoop
wholesale	whisked	whispered	

1. Sue and Al shopped at the ______________ store. ________
2. "______________ should we get for Stu's birthday?" asked Al. ________
3. "How about a ______________ to call his new dog!" ________
4. "______________ are the pet supplies?" asked Al. ________
5. "The ______________ area at the back of the store is for pets," said the salesman. ________
6. "Get a ______________ of that perfume," gagged Sue. ________
7. "Don't insult the people who like it," ______________ Al. ________
8. Sue and Al ______________ through the store quickly and left. ________

Directions Choose the word from the box above which matches each meaning below. Write each word on the line in front of its definition.

1. ______________ a place where ships are docked
2. ______________ a chair which can move from place to place on wheels
3. ______________ a loud shout or cry of joy

Rule The letters **sh**, **ci**, **ce**, and **ti** can stand for the /sh/ sound.

EXAMPLES

Letters	Word	Sound
sh	poli**sh**	/sh/
ci	so**ci**al	/sh/
ce	o**ce**an	/sh/
ti	pa**ti**ence	/sh/

Directions Read each word in the box. Then write it on the line beside its definition.

special diminish Oceania ratio

1. ____________ to make smaller **2.** ____________ proportion

3. ____________ Pacific islands **4.** ____________ distinctive or unique

Directions As you read the story, circle each word that has the /sh/ sound. Then write the words you circled in the correct columns.

Learning about Oceans

Since the days of the ancient Greeks and Phoenicians, people have been interested in exploring the vast oceans that surround us. For a long time people have been nourished by the wide variety of fish, mammals, and crustaceans that inhabit the waters of the earth.

Through patient exploration, we have learned basic information about the make-up of the oceans. Oceanographers have found offshore oil deposits with the potential to help us maintain a sufficient supply of fuel.

ce = /sh/	ti = /sh/	sh = /sh/	ci = /sh/
________	________	________	________
________	________	________	________
________	________	________	________
	________		

Name ______________________________

Directions Read the article. Then circle the letter of the correct answer for each question.

Telephone Features

The first telephone system was not very efficient. Only four people used the same line. No one had a telephone number. People called each other by pushing a knob on the phone.

Over the years, people sought ways to improve the telephone system. Telephones today are a triumph of modern technology. People all over the word can talk to each other.

Some phone features are surprising. For example, if you get a feature called "call forwarding" on your phone, you can dial a code to tell your home telephone where you will be. If someone dials your number, the telephone will ring where you are instead of at your home.

Another bright telephone idea is "automatic callback." With this feature, you can reach a person whose line is busy as soon as he or she hangs up. Your telephone will call you and connect you with the other person when he or she gets off the line.

What will telephones be like in the future? Will people be able to see the person they are talking to? We only know that the phones of the future will be imaginative and even more efficient.

1. The first telephone system was not **efficient.** What does **efficient** mean?
   a. having color b. modern-looking
   c. able to be used without wasting time
2. Telephones are a **triumph** of modern technology. What does **triumph** mean?
   a. oddity b. success c. sad ending
3. Over the years, people **sought** ways to improve the telephone system. What does **sought** mean?
   a. looked for b. forgot about
   c. did not want
4. Another **bright** telephone idea is called "automatic callback." What does **bright** mean in this sentence?
   a. giving much light b. lively and peppy
   c. clever and helpful
5. The phone **system** of tomorrow will be imaginative and efficient. What is a **system?**
   a. a map or graph b. a set of parts that form a whole
   c. showing how something is taken apart

Directions Carefully read the paragraph below. Pay attention to the main ideas.

Hint When you **paraphrase** information, you put it into your own words. In order to paraphrase, you need to understand the most important ideas.

Telephone Etiquette

Telephone etiquette is easy to learn. Suppose you want to call Phil, the neighbor next door. First find the phone number for Phil in the white pages in the phone book. When you have found the number, dial it with patience and care and allow time for Phil to answer. When Phil answers, identify yourself and tell Phil why you are calling. Keep your message brief, because someone else may want to use the telephone. These simple suggestions can make using the phone a pleasure for you, your neighbors, and your friends.

Directions Paraphrase the paragraph above by writing three sentences that give the same information as the long paragraph. On the lines below, write a sentence for each step to follow for placing a telephone call. The first sentence is written for you.

Telephone Etiquette

First, find the number in the white pages of the phone book. ____________________

____

____

____

____

____

____

Name ____________________

Directions The sentences in the paragraphs below include words that have **th**. The sentences are not in the correct sequence. First number each group of sentences in the correct order. Then underline each **th** as in **thin** and circle each **th** as in **then.**

Rule The letters **th** can stand for the /th/ sound as in **thin. Th** can also stand for the /th/ sound as in **then.**

1.

___ Then Mother heard that running is healthful, so she and I joined in.

___ Father really started something when he began to run.

___ First, my brother Matthew began to run with Dad.

___ Now my whole family is so enthusiastic about running that we will enter a marathon on Thursday.

2.

___ "I'd rather go out myself," thought Kim, but she thawed a thick pizza to eat.

___ Mom asked Kim to baby-sit for her baby brother while her family went to the theater.

___ "Thank you a thousand times, Kim," said her mother when they returned, "you're a faithful sister."

___ Later she threw the ball for her brother Seth, who got enthusiastic each time the ball went farther.

Directions Choose two **th** words from the sentences above and use them in an original sentence of your own.

____

____

Rule The letters **sc** can stand for the /sk/, /s/, or /sh/ sounds.

EXAMPLES

Letters	Word	Sound
sc	**sc**alp	/sk/
sc	**sc**ientist	/s/
sc	lu**sc**ious	/sh/

Directions Underline each word in which you see the letters **sc.** Then write /sk/, /s/, or /sh/ above each word you underlined to show the sound that **sc** stands for in that word.

1. At the art museum, we scanned the landscapes first.
2. In one scene, a farmer held a huge scythe.
3. Another view showed a luscious scarlet sunset.
4. In one room we were conscious of the scent of paint.
5. A man on a tall scaffold scowled at us.
6. In the art section, Amy took conscientious notes.
7. I paid scant attention to this school.
8. Many scenes seemed straight from science fiction.
9. But I scampered into the sculpture room to see if they had any work by the sculptor Michelangelo.

Directions Choose a word from those you underlined above to fit each definition.

________________ showing care

________________ glanced at or looked over

________________ moved quickly

________________ smell

________________ pictures of natural inland scenery

________________ frowned

Name ______________________________

Rule The letters **gn** can stand for the /n/ sound as in **resign.** The letters **tch** can stand for the /ch/ sound as in **watch**.

EXAMPLES

Letters	Word	Sound
gn	**gn**at	/n/
tch	ki**tch**en	/ch/

Directions Read the words. Underline each word that contains the letters **gn** and circle each word that contains **tch.**

1. fetched	**2.** watching	**3.** stitched	**4.** batch
5. gnome	**6.** assign	**7.** pitcher	**8.** resign
9. matchless	**10.** kitchen	**11.** gnat	**12.** foreign

Directions Write a word from the box to complete each sentence.

batch	watched	design
sketched	resigned	feigned
	campaign	

1. The artist ______________ a rough drawing on her paper.
2. She had been hired to create a poster for a political ______________.
3. Next she painted a ______________ on a poster board.
4. He cat ______________ her every move.
5. The cat ______________ disinterest, but she hoped to steal a paintbrush.
6. After the artist had made a ______________ of posters, she called it a day.
7. The cat looked ______________ as the artist put her paintbrushes away.

Rule The letters **rh** or **wr** can stand for the /r/ sound.

EXAMPLES

Letters	Word	Sound
rh	**rh**apsody	/r/
wr	**wr**eath	/r/

Directions Write each word from the box beside its definition.

Rhine	wreck	rhubarb
wrath	playwright	wring
rhyme	rhinoceros	overwrought

1. a great anger ________________
2. feeling very upset ________________
3. to squeeze or twist ________________
4. a person who writes plays ________________
5. ruin of a ship or other vehicle ________________
6. having the same sound at the end of words or verses ________________

7. river flowing from Switzerland through Germany, and into the North Sea ________________
8. huge animal with thick skin found in Africa and Asia ________________
9. plant with thick stalks that can be cooked or baked ________________

Directions Complete each sentence by choosing the correct word from the box above.

1. The ________________ has written many plays about her adventures.
2. One play is set on the ________________ River in Germany.
3. In another, she describes the ________________ of a famous steamship.
4. Three of her plays are written in ________________ rather than prose.
5. Toward critics, she feels nothing but ________________.
6. "I'd like to ________________ his neck," she said of one critic.

Name ____________________

Rule The letters **ear** can stand for the /ear/ sound, but sometimes **ear** stands for the /air/ sound or the /ur/ sound.

Examples

Letters	Word	Sound
ear	app**ear**	/ear/
ear	w**ear**	/air/
ear	s**ear**ch	/ur/

Directions Write **ear, pear,** or **pearl** to show which sound the letters **ear** stand for.

1. weary ____________ 2. earnest ____________ 3. spear ____________
4. earth ____________ 5. tear ____________ 6. clear ____________
7. gears ____________ 8. learn ____________ 9. bearer ____________
10. smear ____________ 11. beard ____________ 12. earrings ____________

Directions Think of a word that fits each definition and has the sound of **ear** shown at the top of the column. Write the word in the boxes at the right.

ear as in **ear**

1. a feeling of terror or fright
2. opposite of *far*
3. twelve months
4. to listen to sounds

f e a r

ear as in **pear**

1. a large mammal with thick fur
2. to have on the body
3. to become torn
4. person or thing that carries

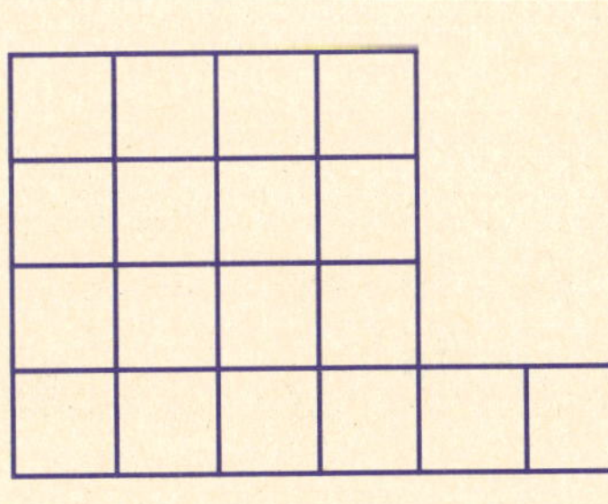

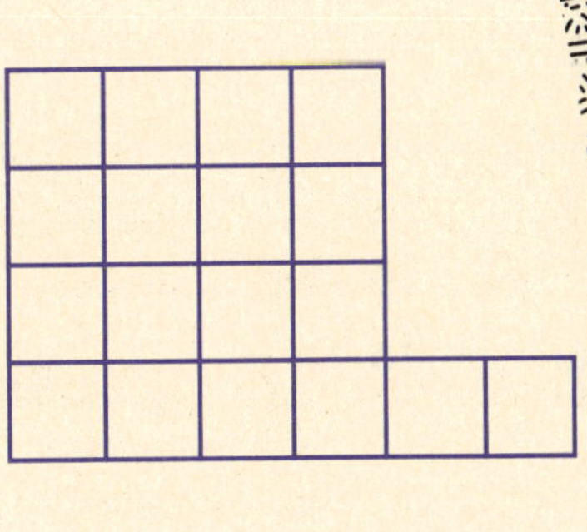

ear as in **pearl**

1. listened to
2. to look for
3. to gain knowledge
4. planet we live on

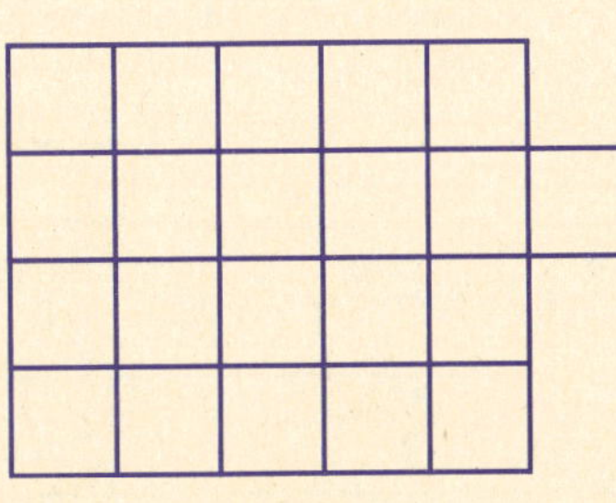

Directions Write a word from the box that fits each definition.

rehearsal	bearded	earthenware
yearling	bearings	research
spearmint	forebears	rainwear

1. a plant used for flavoring ____________________
2. a one-year-old animal ____________________
3. practice for a play or speech ____________________
4. clothes for wet weather ____________________
5. people who lived before us ____________________
6. dishes or jars made from baked clay ____________________
7. careful reading and study to find out information ____________________
8. having hair growing on the lower part of the face ____________________
9. direction or position of something, as a ship's ____________________

Directions Write the letter of the phrase that completes each sentence. Then circle each word that contains **ear** and write the word in the correct column.

____ 1. This year we will go
____ 2. We'll pack our gear and decide
____ 3. Last trip we heard
____ 4. We learned to stay quiet,
____ 5. Clearly we must travel east to
____ 6. Will we earn any points

a. a bear.
b. what to wear.
c. if we don't tear our clothes?
d. get our bearings.
e. camping with Earth Trails.
f. so we had no fear.

ear as in **appear**	**ear** as in **wear**	**ear** as in **search**
____________	____________	____________
____________	____________	____________
____________	____________	____________
____________	____________	____________

Name ______________________________

Rule The letters **air** and **are** can stand for the /air/ sound.

EXAMPLES

Letters	Word	Sound
air	**pair**	/air/
are	sc**are**	/air/

Directions Use the words from the box to complete the rhymes.

repair	fair	rare
declare	Blair	flair
despair	care	air

There once was a young boy named ____________,
Who one day was heard to ____________,
"I'll inflate a balloon,
While I'm singing a tune!"
Was young Blair just full of hot ____________?

There was a sad girl in ____________,
Who wanted to go to the ____________.
She got there by noon,
And then very soon,
She felt like she hadn't a ____________.

There once was a man with a ____________,
Who could do any kind of ____________.
He fixed odds and ends,
For all of his friends.
They agreed that his talent was ____________.

Directions Fill in the circle beside the word that completes each sentence.

1. The day dawned sunny and ____ on our farm.
   ❍ cost ❍ cold ❍ mold

2. We planned to ____ a large birthday party that evening.
   ❍ host ❍ ghost ❍ most

3. Grandma was seventy years ____.
   ❍ told ❍ old ❍ kind

4. Then the ____ weather grew violent.
   ❍ kind ❍ hold ❍ mild

5. A ____ blizzard sprang up and covered the land.
   ❍ wind ❍ wild ❍ gold

6. "There will be no letters from the ____ office today," said Grandmother.
   ❍ find ❍ fold ❍ post

7. "No, the carrier would get ____ in the snow and wind," replied Grandpa.
   ❍ lost ❍ most ❍ mind

8. "How will people ____ us for the party?" asked Katya.
   ❍ hind ❍ find ❍ grind

9. "I doubt anyone will get through," Grandpa ____ her.
   ❍ told ❍ bold ❍ sold

10. "We will ____ another party in the spring," laughed Mother.
    ❍ mold ❍ cold ❍ hold

11. By morning, ____ of the high winds had stopped.
    ❍ most ❍ ghost ❍ mild

12. The sunlight on the snow looked like ____.
    ❍ ghost ❍ gold ❍ mild

13. Katya thought the bright sun might ____ her.
    ❍ sold ❍ child ❍ blind

Name ______________________________

Directions Read each word in the list. Write the number of syllables. Then write the word in the correct column.

Hint If you hear one vowel sound in a word, the word has one syllable. If you hear two vowel sounds, the word has two syllables, and so on.

1.	___	appear	**2.**	___	share			
3.	___	repairing	**4.**	___	thunder			
5.	___	calm	**6.**	___	bindings	**7.**	___	flair
8.	___	sympathetic	**9.**	___	earring	**10.**	___	celebration
11.	___	youth	**12.**	___	astonishment	**13.**	___	authentic
14.	___	proficient	**15.**	___	mathematics	**16.**	___	carefully

One Syllable	**Two Syllables**
______________	______________
______________	______________
______________	______________
______________	______________

Three Syllables	**Four Syllables**
______________	______________
______________	______________
______________	______________
______________	______________

Directions Study the rules. Then, divide the words into syllables using vertical lines.

Rule	Examples	
Rule When two or more consonants come between two vowels in a word, the word is usually divided between the first two consonants.	bet/ter per/mit	wes/tern big/ger
Rule When a single consonant comes between two vowels in a word, the word is usually divided after the consonant if the first vowel is short.	nev/er shad/ow	Phil/ip rap/id
Rule When a single consonant comes between two vowels in a word, the word is usually divided before the consonant if the first vowel is long.	po/lar ra/zor	na/tion hu/mor
Rule When a consonant blend or consonant digraph comes between two vowels in a word, the word is usually divided after the blend or digraph if the first vowel is short, or before the blend or digraph if the first vowel is long.	moth/er tick/et	di/graph ze/bra

1. earnest ________ **2.** nectar ________ **3.** sentence ________

4. object ________ **5.** cartoon ________ **6.** shoulder ________

7. reward ________ **8.** photo ________ **9.** jacket ________

10. shiver ________ **11.** comic ________ **12.** either ________

13. rhubarb ________ **14.** cricket ________ **15.** quiver ________

16. brother ________ **17.** cabin ________ **18.** cheetah ________

Name ______________________________

Directions Write the correct word from the box to complete each unfinished sentence.

their	early	year	physical
Greece	wreath	fair	written
race	Wrestling	fighting	eighty

The Olympics Then and Now

The first recorded Olympic Games were held in Greece in the ______________ (1) 776 B.C. During that time, all the citizens of ______________ (2) would agree to a one-month truce from ______________ (3).

The Greeks held those ______________ (4) Games to honor ______________ (5) gods. The Greeks thought the ______________ (6) tests of strength would please Zeus.

The only event in the ancient Olympics was a ______________ (7). Records show that a man named Coroebus won the first race. He was crowned with an olive ______________ (8), which was a sign of peace. Poems and songs were ______________ (9) to honor the winners of the Games.

In later years, other events were added to the competition. ______________ (10) and track and field events were included. The judges that decided the winners of the events had to be honest and ______________ (11).

Modern Olympic Games are held every four years in different places in the world. At that time athletes from more than ______________ (12) nations compete against one another as the whole world watches.

Directions Suppose you are a good enough athlete to train for the Olympic Games. Put a check by the event you would choose, or write your own idea.

________	swimming	________	hockey	________	diving
________	marathon	________	track and field	________	skiing
________	wrestling	________	bobsledding	________	basketball
________	gymnastics	________	ice skating	________ (your idea)	

Directions Use the words in the box to answer the questions. Be sure to answer each question with a complete sentence.

dare	earnest	healthy	year	wear
careful	fair	youth	weary	athletic

1. Why did you choose this sport?

____

____

2. What qualities does a person need to succeed in this sport?

____

____

3. What types of clothing and equipment are needed?

____

____

4. How long and how often does a person need to practice the sport?

____

____

5. Who are some famous athletes that are good at this sport?

____

____

Name ______________________________

Directions Write a word from the box to correctly complete each sentence. Use each word only once.

Rule The vowel digraphs **ai** and **ay** can stand for the /ā/ sound in **paint** and **may.**

waited	stay	playful	acquaintances
mayor	Saturday	explain	rain

1. Over two hundred citizens gathered at the park last ______________.
2. The ______________ was scheduled to make an important announcement.
3. He wanted to ______________ the plans for building a new town library.
4. The crowd ______________ patiently for the chief official to arrive.
5. Some people were feeling ______________ and organized a ball game.
6. Others were content to chat with old ______________.
7. It began to ______________ before the mayor arrived.
8. Many people did not ______________ to hear his proclamation.

Directions Underline each word in which **ai** stands for the /ā/ sound. Circle each word in which **ay** stands for the /ā/ sound.

waist	baste	may
paisley	gnats	pastel
bay	bait	mayor
crayon	flail	paid
archway	daily	relay
Saturday	taste	train
sailboat	scallops	faith
diagram	exclaim	dainty
playwright	braid	delay

Directions Read each word. Write the word from the box that means the opposite.

gain	display	fail	plain	playful	rainy
decay	daytime	stay	afraid	delay	daily

1. ______________ ornate
2. ______________ brave
3. ______________ conceal
4. ______________ leave
5. ______________ serious
6. ______________ nightly
7. ______________ nighttime
8. ______________ pass
9. ______________ sunny
10. ______________ thrive
11. ______________ begin
12. ______________ lose

Directions Each word in the list names something that moves people or things. Read each definition. Then write the letter of the correct definition by each word.

___ **1.** monorail **a.** the part of a road used by vehicles

___ **2.** railway **b.** an electric railroad running below the surface of city streets

___ **3.** driveway **c.** narrow back street in a city or town

___ **4.** roadway **d.** paved strip of land at an airport on which aircraft take off and land

___ **5.** alleyway **e.** path for cars that leads from a road to a garage or house

___ **6.** runway **f.** track made of rails

___ **7.** subway **g.** train that moves along on one rail

Name ____________________

Directions Circle the letters that stand for the /ē/ sound.

Rule The vowel digraphs **ee** and **ei** can stand for the /ē/ sound you hear in **bee** and **ceiling.**

1. three	**2.** leisure	**3.** dungarees
4. proceed	**5.** seizure	**6.** weekly
7. conceit	**8.** protein	**9.** pedigree
10. sheik	**11.** marquee	**12.** neither
13. steeple	**14.** breeze	**15.** jubilee

Directions Use a word from the list above to answer each riddle.

1. Found in such foods
As eggs, milk, and meat,
It helps build strong bones,
From our head to our feet.

What is it? ____________________

2. If you want to know
The name of the show,
Look on the sign
With its lights aglow.

What is it? ____________________

3. The chief of a village,
A tribe, or a clan,
An Arabian ruler,
He's a powerful man.

Who is he? ____________________

4. Best of the breed and winner of fame,
Sometimes a dog has papers that name
The ancestry from which it came.

What is it? ____________________

5. One plus two,
Four minus one,
Solve either problem.
The riddle is done.

What is the answer? ____________________

Directions Find words in the puzzle that have the vowel digraph **ee** or **ei.** Some go across, and others go down. Circle each word you find. Then write the word in the correct column.

E	I	T	H	E	R	B	C	D	A	Z	L	M	N	G
B	O	E	B	F	E	E	T	L	R	X	Y	J	M	T
D	R	I	F	G	C	P	N	M	L	F	G	D	B	C
T	H	T	G	R	E	E	D	N	H	A	F	R	E	E
L	C	H	G	L	I	Z	M	S	U	C	C	E	E	D
M	C	P	C	Z	P	H	X	E	Y	F	R	C	A	E
O	U	B	C	D	T	R	E	E	T	G	M	E	Z	C
A	B	Z	Y	X	W	Z	N	M	K	R	A	I	Y	E
C	M	T	G	H	J	K	L	S	T	Z	B	V	W	I
Z	T	G	M	C	V	O	E	R	N	W	M	E	E	T

ee words

ei words

______	______	______
______	______	______
______	______	______
______	______	______

Directions Write a word you found in the puzzle to complete each sentence.

1. I hope that I ______ a good grade on my paper.
2. I should get ______ an A or a B.
3. It ______ like I spent a month writing it!
4. I know it takes hard work to ______!

Name ____

Directions Fill in the circle beside the word that completes each sentence.

Rule The vowel digraphs **oa, oe,** and **ow** can stand for the /ō/ sound as in **loan, toe,** and **flow.**

1. Jack is an athletic boy who is always ____ of his talents.
   ❍ floating ❍ boasting ❍ outgrowing

2. He told everyone when he got three strikes the last time he went ____.
   ❍ floating ❍ glowing ❍ bowling

3. He made an announcement when he shot the ____ into the center of the target.
   ❍ mistletoe ❍ minnow ❍ arrow

4. He ____ when he hit two home runs in the baseball game.
   ❍ coached ❍ gloated ❍ coaxed

5. He even notified the newspaper when he scored the most ____ on his soccer team.
   ❍ goals ❍ toes ❍ glows

6. Most of Jack's classmates ____ when he begins talking.
   ❍ grow ❍ toe ❍ groan

7. Some ____ away so they won't have to listen.
   ❍ outgrow ❍ throat ❍ tiptoe

8. Others ____ up their hands in disgust.
   ❍ tow ❍ toe ❍ throw

9. Even the ____ is getting tired of Jack's attitude.
   ❍ loaves ❍ bowstring ❍ coach

10. He gets a ____ look on his face when he hears Jack start to brag.
    ❍ woeful ❍ outgrow ❍ stowaway

Directions Write the word from the box that names each picture. Then circle the letters that stand for the /ō/ sound.

wheelbarrow	doe	crowbar	toaster
coach	elbow	loaves	tiptoe
arrow	goal	float	bowling

Name ____

Directions Read the article. Complete each unfinished word by filling in the vowel digraph **ai, ay, ee, ei, oa, oe,** or **ow.**

The End of Pompeii

The Roman city of Pompeii was located near the Bay of Naples in southern Italy, less than a mile aw__1__ from the volcano, Mount Vesuvius. In its early d__2__s, Pompeii was a simple village, with only a few inhabitants. In time, Pompeii's pleasant scenery and agr__3__able climate attracted wealthy Romans to the city. By the first century A.D., the c__4__stal city of Pompeii had become a prosperous, gr__5__ing community, b__6__sting large homes, a busy marketplace, and several theaters for entert__7__nment.

To the dism__8__ of the citizens, Mount Vesuvius erupted in A.D. 63. Pompeii and several nearby towns suffered damage. The residents quickly repaired their homes, thinking that Vesuvius would not erupt again.

Then in A.D. 79, Vesuvius erupted with even more violence than before. Lava and mud flowed from the volcano so quickly that few people had time to escape. Hot ashes, cinders, and stones thr__9__n into the air by the volcano rained down on the city. Soon, r__10__ds were t__11__ming with people fl__12__ing for their lives.

Few were able to escape. Thousands of people were killed by falling stones and cinders or by poisonous fumes that came from the volcano. Others were trapped in their homes, crushed by falling c__13__lings and walls. Even those who succ__14__ded in getting outside were not safe. Debris was falling into the narr__15__ str__16__ts.

The ashes and cinders that covered and destroyed Pompeii also preserved it. When they cooled, these ashes and cinders formed a layer that sealed up the city buried below. The archaeologists who discovered the ruins much later found Pompeii just as the people had left it on the day Vesuvius erupted.

Directions This is your chance to practice good writing skills. Read the sentences and number them in the correct order. Then write each paragraph so the sentences tell the events that happened in the city of Pompeii in the correct sequence.

Hint Good writers revise their work by checking to see that what they wrote is well organized. They ask questions such as: Is everything in its proper place? Are items and events described in the correct sequence, or order?

Paragraph 1

___ The inhabitants of Pompeii quickly rebuilt their homes and streets.

___ They were sure the volcano would cause no further damage.

___ Mount Vesuvius erupted briefly in A.D. 63.

Paragraph 2

___ Then the hot ashes, cinders, and stones thrown into the air above the volcano rained down on the city of Pompeii.

___ However in A.D. 79, Vesuvius erupted again, with even more violence than before.

___ The eruption caused liquid lava and mud to pour into the town so quickly that few people had time to escape.

Name ______________________________

Rule The vowel digraph **ea** can stand for the /ā/ sound you hear in the word **steak**, the /ē/ sound in **meat**, or the /e/ sound in **bread**.

Examples

Letters	Word	Sound
ea	break	/ā/
ea	wheat	/ē/
ea	thread	/e/

Directions Write the word from the box that names each picture. Then circle the vowel sound you hear.

breakfast	steak	feather
wheat	seal	leash
pheasant	thread	break

1. /ā/ /ē/ /e/

____

2. /ā/ /ē/ /e/

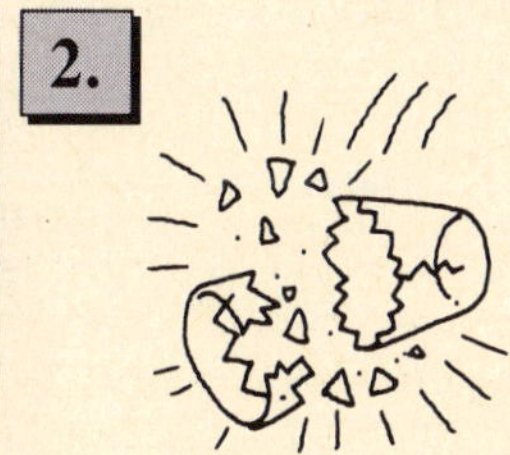

____

3. /ā/ /ē/ /e/

____

4. /ā/ /ē/ /e/

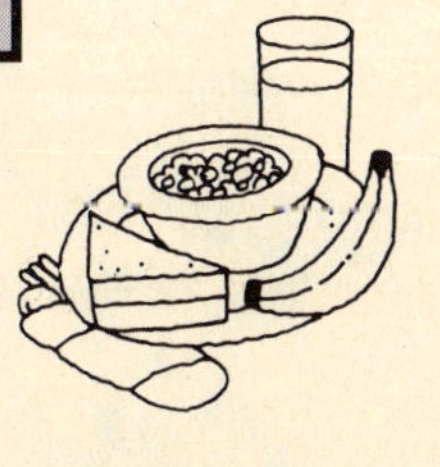

____

5. /ā/ /ē/ /e/

____

6. /ā/ /ē/ /e/

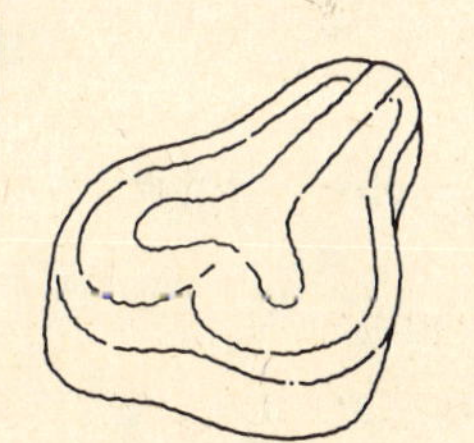

____

7. /ā/ /ē/ /e/

____

8. /ā/ /ē/ /e/

____

9. /ā/ /ē/ /e/

____

Directions Use the words in the box to answer the questions. Use each word only once. Write /ā/, /ē/, or /e/ beside each word you write to show the sound of **ea.**

steak	beagle	feathers	pleasant	wheat
break	thread	jealous	leash	beaver

1. Which word means the same as *envious?*

 ____

2. Which word means an ingredient in bread?

 ____

3. What might you use to walk your dog?

 ____

4. What would you use to sew a rip in your shirt?

 ____

5. Which word names a kind of meat?

 ____

6. What is another name for a small dog with drooping ears?

 ____

7. How could you describe a day that went well?

 ____

8. Which word means the same as *smash?*

 ____

9. What animal is known for building dams?

 ____

10. What covers the bodies of birds?

 ____

Name ____________________

Rule The vowel digraph **ie** can stand for the /ē/ sound in the word **field** or the /ī/ sound in **pie**.

EXAMPLES

Letters	Word	Sound
ie	ch**ie**f	/ē/
ie	t**ie**d	/ī/

Directions Read the story. Circle each word in which the vowel digraph **ie** sounds like /ē/. Draw a line under each word in which **ie** sounds like /ī/.

Our Eventful Day

My brother and I wanted to drive the family car to the parade downtown, but Dad said, "No." We begged, but he would not yield, so we had to take the bus. We thought we would have a brief wait. Instead, we stood for an unbelievably long time at the bus stop. When the bus finally arrived, the driver apologized to the dissatisfied people. "I'm sorry this bus is late," he said. "Traffic was all tied up because of an accident."

As we got off the bus, two girls dashed past us shrieking and yelling, "Zeke! Stop! Someone grab our dog! His leash broke." We tried to catch the little dog, but he soon disappeared, shielded by the crowd.

In spite of the confusion, we were on time for the parade. It was really exciting. The mayor led the parade. The fire chief drove a 1928 fire engine. Marching bands, led by girls wielding batons, vied for first place in the band competition. Clowns laughed and cried and performed tricks in the streets. We watched in disbelief as unicyclists applied their skill on the one-wheeled bikes. Some of the unicycles were so tall that their riders towered close to the traffic lights and street lamps.

After the parade we stopped to eat. My brother had French fried mushrooms, while I had lemon pie. All of a sudden, we spied the dog, Zeke, that had run away from the girls. He was sitting on the sidewalk looking at us through the window of the restaurant. We notified the police, who had the address of the owner.

Luckily for us, the owner of the dog was so relieved that she sent us a reward. If Dad had let us use the car, we would not have helped retrieve the dog. Then we would not be twenty-five dollars richer either. We really were more than satisfied.

Directions Circle the vowel digraph **ie** in each word. Write /ī/ if **ie** stands for the long **i** sound. Write /ē/ if **ie** stands for the long **e** sound.

1.	yield	______	**2.**	cried	______
3.	satisfied	______	**4.**	brief	______
5.	unbelievable	______	**6.**	fried	______
7.	shrieking	______	**8.**	disbelief	______
9.	chief	______	**10.**	fields	______

Directions Write a word from the list to complete each unfinished sentence.

1. Before the Pilgrims left the ship they signed a ______________ agreement about the rules of the new settlement.
2. The eyes of the Pilgrims widened in ______________ when they saw the deep forest and abundance of wild animals.
3. The Indian ______________ promised his tribe would help the settlers plant their crops.
4. The settlers of Plymouth worked hard to make sure the land would ______________ enough food.
5. When all the crops had been harvested, the Pilgrims were more than ______________ with their work.
6. ______________ cornmeal mush was prepared over the campfires.
7. The little Pilgrim children began ______________ in excitement when they saw the dinner being prepared.
8. Although they were happy in their new land, it is hard for us to imagine all the ______________ problems they lived with in the New World.

Name ______________________________

Rule The vowel digraphs **ei** and **ey** can stand for the /ā/ sound.

EXAMPLES

Letters	Word	Sound
ei	r**ei**n	/ā/
ey	ob**ey**	/ā/

Directions Use the words in the box to work the crossword puzzle.

vein	reign	they	disobey	prey	obey
skein	whey	rein	survey	convey	reindeer

Across

3. animal found in Greenland and some countries in northern Europe
4. to deliberately go against the command of a superior
7. strap attached to a bridle
10. thin, watery part of milk that appears when cheese is made
11. to take from one place to another

Down

1. loose coil of yarn
2. to measure land
3. to rule over a country
5. to do what one is told
6. an animal that is hunted
8. a blood vessel that carries blood to the heart
9. a pronoun to describe persons, animals, or things

Directions Circle the correct word to complete each sentence. Then write the word on the line.

Rule The vowel digraphs **au** and **aw** can stand for the vowel sound you hear in **auto** and **claws.**

1. It was a blustery day and a (law, raw) wind was blowing. ____________
2. Cars and floats (caught, crawled) along the parade route. ____________
3. A celebrity waved from a shiny white (authority, automobile). ____________
4. Her sequined (shawl, straw) sparkled in the sunlight. ____________
5. Fans pushed through the crowd to get her (autograph, automatic). ____________
6. The star (cautioned, scrawled) her name for her admirers. ____________
7. Later she had a conference with her (laundry, lawyer). ____________
8. He (cautioned, haunted) her to review her contract carefully. ____________
9. This rising young star often (fawns, flaunts) her success. ____________
10. Her critics describe her as being (haughty, awning). ____________

Name ____________________

Directions Read the article. Then write the correct word from the box to complete each unfinished sentence.

laws	dried	libraries	authorities
Eastern	heavy	scrawling	great
breakable	chief	discoveries	read

Early Writing

If you had been going to school in the seventh century B.C., in the Near ____________ (1) land of Mesopotamia, you might have wanted to study in one of the ____________ (2). Instead of reading a book, you would have ____________ (3) clay tablets containing strange markings called *cuneiform writing.*

In Mesopotamia, people "wrote" with an instrument called a stylus. They would scratch or press wedge-shaped marks into damp clay. The rectangular clay tablets were then ____________ (4) in the sun or baked in an oven until they were hard.

How were the tablets used and what was written on them? The people of Mesopotamia used the tablets for recording a ____________ (5) many different kinds of messages. Government ____________ (6) used some tablets to record ____________ (7) and rules.

Using the tablets could be difficult. Because the tablets had to dry for several hours, writing was never simply a matter of ____________ (8) down a message and sending it through the mail.

One of the ____________ (9) problems was the size and weight of the tablets. This made them too bulky and ____________ (10) to be easily carried from place to place. Storing the large tablets also was difficult, especially because the clay was brittle and quite ____________ (11). Because of these problems, the bulky tablets were stored in libraries.

One of the greatest ____________ (12) of cuneiform inscriptions was the library of Nineveh, containing 25,000 tablets. This great library was established in the seventh century B.C., as a result of the endeavors of King Assurbanipal.

Hint Revising what you have written gives you a chance to make your work more interesting and exciting to the reader.

When you read over what you have written, ask yourself:

Have I used some words too often?

Can I use different words to make my writing give the reader a better picture?

Can I think of other interesting details to help the reader better understand what I am trying to say?

Directions Read each pair of sentences. Circle the number of the sentence that gives a better picture.

1. People in ancient Mesopotamia scratched messages onto clay tablets.

2. In Mesopotamia people wrote messages on tablets.

---

1. The heavy clay tablets were too large to carry easily and a problem to store because they were breakable.

2. The tablets were heavy and not easy to store.

Directions Use details from the article on page 41 to revise the paragraph and make it more interesting.

In Mesopotamia, the difficulties of putting messages on tablets led to some of the earliest libraries. The clay tablets had to have time to dry. Also, the tablets were heavy and hard to carry. Another problem was that the tablets were breakable. Storing the tablets in libraries helped solve these problems.

Name ______________________________

Rule The vowel digraph **oo** can stand for the /o͞o/ sound as in **goose**, the /o͝o/ sound as in **look**, or the /u/ sound as in **blood**.

Examples

Letters	Word	Sound
oo	boot	/o͞o/
oo	foot	/o͝o/
oo	flood	/u/

Directions Show the sound that the vowel digraph **oo** stands for in each word. Write /o͞o/, /o͝o/, or /u/ on the line.

1. swoop ________ **2.** snoop ________ **3.** nook ________

4. brook ________ **5.** moody ________ **6.** swoon ________

7. tycoon ________ **8.** floodlight ________ **9.** neighborhood ________

10. moose ________ **11.** stood ________ **12.** loot ________

13. bassoon ________ **14.** bloodless ________ **15.** schooner ________

Directions Read the list of make-believe mystery cases. Circle each word that has the digraph **oo.** Then write each circled word in the correct column.

1. The Clue of the Snowy Footprints in the Woods
2. The Case of the Missing Driftwood in Gloomy Lagoon
3. The Mystery of the Crooked Footpath at Moonbeam Hill
4. The Missing Heirloom of Doom
5. The Bloodhound that Discovered the Pirates of Greenwood
6. The Case of the Gold Doubloons

oo as in **look**

________ ________ ________

________ ________ ________

oo as in **boot**

________ ________ ________

________ ________ ________

oo as in **flood**

____

Directions Read each definition and look at the vowel sound beside it. Then write the word that matches the definition and contains the vowel sound shown by the symbol in front of the line.

1. a small furry animal with a long, bushy ringed tail /o͞o/ ____________________
2. soft covering for the head /o͝o/ ____________________
3. small cage or pen for chickens /o͞o/ ____________________
4. stack of wood /o͝o/ ____________________
5. male chicken /o͞o/ ____________________
6. a heavenly body that revolves around the earth and shines at night /o͞o/ ____________________
7. a large dog with a keen sense of smell /u/ ____________________
8. mark made by a foot /o͝o/ ____________________
9. a swimming bird similar to a duck /o͞o/ ____________________
10. covering for foot and lower leg /o͞o/ ____________________

Name ____________________

Rule The vowel digraph **ui** can stand for the /i/ sound you hear in **guilt** or the /o͞o/ sound you hear in **cruise**.

EXAMPLES

Letters	Word	Sound
ui	b**ui**ld	/i/
ui	j**ui**ce	/o͞o/

Directions Read each sentence. Underline the words in which **ui** sounds like the **ui** in **bruise** and circle the words in which **ui** sounds like the **ui** in **guilty.** Then categorize the words at the bottom.

1. My father just built a new restaurant.
2. The unusual building attracts many customers.
3. It was designed to look like a cruise ship.
4. Patrons must wear suitable clothing.
5. Bathing suits are not allowed.
6. The specialty is thick, juicy steaks.
7. The crisp, light biscuits are in demand.
8. The fresh fruit salad is also very popular.
9. Customers enjoy listening to the guitar music.
10. No one ever causes a nuisance.

bruise	guilty
____________	____________
____________	____________
____________	____________
____________	____________
____________	
____________	

Directions Choose a word from the box that correctly completes each unfinished sentence.

nuisance	suits	cruising	suitably
building	guilty	pursuit	build

1. Two men hastily left the ________________ and raced down the street.
2. They were dressed in black ________________ and were carrying a small bag.
3. One man was heavyset and the other had a much leaner ________________.
4. They made so much noise that they were quite a ________________.
5. A police car was ________________ in the area at that precise moment.
6. The police hurried off in ________________ of the two suspects.
7. When they caught the men, it was obvious that they were ________________.
8. Most likely they will be ________________ punished for their crime.

Directions Underline the words in which **ui** sounds like the **ui** in **build** and circle the words in which **ui** sounds like the **ui** in **juice.**

fruit	mannequins	biscuits	exquisite
circuit	cruise	suitable	quilt
built	guitar	guilty	bruise
pursuit	recruit	cruiser	building

Name ____________________

Directions Read the words in the box. Then read the paragraphs below. Write the word from the box that correctly completes each unfinished sentence.

wool	roof	harpoons	juices
fruits	blood	suited	built
livelihood	footbridges	food	good

The Great Inca Empire

Several thousand years ago, a group of primitive Indians living in South America earned their ____________ (1) by hunting and fishing. Their weapons were bows and arrows, sticks, and ____________ (2). Little by little, those primitive Indians developed into the great Empire of the Incas. By the time the Spaniards came to the New World, the Incas were the most advanced and the best known of all the Indian tribes in South America. Their capital city of Cuzco, Peru, was so high up in the mountains that the Incas were said to be living on the " ____________ (3) of the world."

Because of the high altitude, weather was extremely cold. Clothing ____________ (4) to the climate was made from the ____________ (5) of the alpaca or the llama. However, the Inca ruler and those of noble ____________ (6) wore clothes made from the fleece of the vicuña. The Incas who lived along the coast did not need heavy, warm clothes. They made clothing of the cotton which they wove and then dyed with the ____________ (7) of berries and certain ____________ (8) and vegetables.

The rulers were ____________ (9) to their people. They tried to make them happy, giving them land on which to grow enough ____________ (10).

The Incas were skillful farmers. They not only farmed the mountain valleys, but also planted crops on the terraces which they had ____________ (11) on the steep mountainsides. Canals and ditches carried water from the mountain streams to irrigate the fields.

There were many talented engineers among the Incas. Suspension bridges, built by the engineers, still look the same as they did centuries ago. Some of these ____________ (12) are still used by people living in remote areas. Gigantic Inca ruins still stand today in many parts of Peru.

Directions Pretend you are a newspaper reporter living thousands of years ago in South America. You have discovered the Inca Indians, and want to write an article about them. Use the main ideas listed in the box below to write a three paragraph article about the Incas. Be sure the sentences in each paragraph support the main idea. If they do not, rewrite the sentences or leave them out.

An advanced Indian tribe is found living in Peru.
The Incas are skillful farmers.
The Incas are also good engineers.

Name ____________________

Definition A diphthong consists of two vowels blended together to make one sound.

EXAMPLES

The diphthongs **oi** and **oy** stand for the same sound. They stand for the vowel sound you hear in **coin** and **boy**.

Directions Read each word. Circle the diphthong **oi** or **oy.** Then write the word from the box that matches the definition.

recoil	corduroy	turquoise	royalty	poison
spoil	ointment	embroidery	moisten	asteroids
annoy	turmoil	sequoia	loyalty	exploit
voyage	foible	viceroy	enjoyable	embroil

1. small planets that revolve around the sun between Mars and Jupiter

 ____

2. greenish-blue stone used for jewelry

 ____

3. a thick cotton cloth with velvetlike ridges

 ____

4. to bother

 ____

5. to involve in trouble or conflict

 ____

6. bold, unusual act; daring deed

 ____

7. an evergreen tree that can grow to be very tall, like the redwood

 ____

8. those who have the powers of a king or queen

 ____

Definition An **analogy** tells the relationship that one thing has to another thing.

EXAMPLE

Racquet is to **tennis** as **bat** is to **ball**.

Directions Circle the correct ending for each analogy and write it on the line.

1. **Asteroid** is to **sun** as **moon** is to ________________.
   loyal   earth   enjoy
2. **Corduroy** is to **pants** as **turquoise** is to ________________.
   annoy   toil   ring
3. **Brush** is to **painting** as **needle** is to ________________.
   embroidery   ointment   moist
4. **Airplane** is to **flight** as **ship** is to ________________.
   loyalty   voyage   recoil
5. **Strawberry** is to **fruit** as **redwood** is to ________________.
   foil   spoil   sequoia
6. **Queen** is to **royalty** as **dime** is to ________________.
   coin   join   noisemaker
7. **Noisemaker** is to **noisy** as **glue** is to ________________.
   enjoyed   boiled   joined

Directions Complete this analogy.

Soil is to **garden** as **water** is to ______________________________.

Name ______________________________

Directions Read each word in the box. Circle the diphthong **ou** or **ow.** Then write the word from the box that names each picture.

Rule The diphthongs **ou** and **ow** often stand for the vowel sound in **out** and **scowl.**

trowel	sow	sunflower	trout
mountain	bow	brow	pound
hound	vowels	countess	scout
fountain	south	plow	owl

1.

____

2.

____

3.

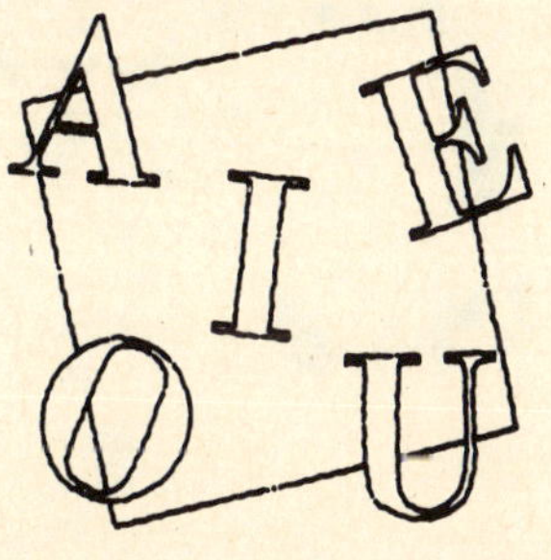

____

4.

____

5.

____

6.

____

Directions Read the words in each row. Draw a line under the two words that have the same vowel sound. Then circle the letters that stand for the sound.

1.	cowl	foul	glamour
2.	devout	four	grouch
3.	pout	growl	dough
4.	tower	sew	renown
5.	owe	out	powder
6.	chowder	soup	mountain
7.	touch	prowl	towel
8.	cowboy	bounty	dozen
9.	scowl	enormous	fowl
10.	journey	frown	profound
11.	eyebrow	crouch	coupon
12.	soupy	snout	allowance
13.	recount	how	flown
14.	endow	tough	shout
15.	doubt	cougar	coward

Directions Write a phrase from the box to answer each question.

loud crowd	hound sound
cow chow	shower flower

1. What would you call the howl from a hunting dog? __________
2. What would you call a very noisy group of people? __________
3. What would you call feed for a herd of cattle? __________
4. What would you call a plant that blooms only when it rains? __________

Name ______________________________

Directions Complete the crossword puzzle by finding the **ew** word in the box that fits each description.

Rule The diphthong **ew** stands for the vowel sound in **few.** It is nearly the same vowel sound you hear in **moon.**

renewal	newspaper	few	shrewd	steward	mildew
flew	pewter	dew	drew	nephew	chew
jeweler	crew	yew	blew	views	new

Across

4. what you do to food before swallowing it
5. person who makes, sells, or repairs necklaces and watches
8. making something new or fresh again
9. clever or wise
11. kind of furry, white fungus that appears during damp weather
12. type of evergreen tree or shrub

Down

1. sheets of paper telling the news of the day
2. a grayish metal made by mixing tin with lead, brass, or copper
3. opposite of *many*
4. group of sailors working on a ship
6. the son of a person's sister or brother
7. past tense of *fly*
10. past tense of *draw*

Directions Write the number of syllables you hear in each word. Then write the vowel digraph or diphthong.

		Syllables Heard	Digraph or Diphthong			Syllables Heard	Digraph or Diphthong
1.	juice	______	______	**2.**	woodpecker	______	______
3.	fellows	______	______	**4.**	account	______	______
5.	counter	______	______	**6.**	treason	______	______
7.	reign	______	______	**8.**	pheasant	______	______
9.	down	______	______	**10.**	retrieve	______	______
11.	portray	______	______	**12.**	survey	______	______
13.	treat	______	______	**14.**	dauntless	______	______
15.	waterproof	______	______	**16.**	withdrew	______	______
17.	disobey	______	______	**18.**	seamstress	______	______
19.	treachery	______	______	**20.**	reasonable	______	______
21.	sluice	______	______	**22.**	occupied	______	______
23.	essay	______	______	**24.**	board	______	______
25.	thesaurus	______	______	**26.**	gingerbread	______	______
27.	breaker	______	______	**28.**	mayhem	______	______
29.	withdraw	______	______	**30.**	thundercloud	______	______
31.	refugee	______	______	**32.**	greedy	______	______
33.	schoolmaster	______	______	**34.**	growth	______	______
35.	author	______	______	**36.**	however	______	______
37.	soapy	______	______	**38.**	tomorrow	______	______
39.	oboe	______	______	**40.**	upheaval	______	______
41.	shower	______	______	**42.**	feast	______	______
43.	applause	______	______	**44.**	appoint	______	______
45.	shook	______	______	**46.**	hawthorn	______	______
47.	renew	______	______	**48.**	authentic	______	______

Name ______________________________

Directions Read the article. Complete each unfinished word by writing one of the diphthongs **oi, oy, ew, ou,** or **ow.** Then write each word you completed in the correct column.

Alexander the Great

By the time he was thirty years old, Alexander the Great had conquered most of the ancient civilized world. In less than fifteen years, Alexander and his troops had overp_____(1)ered the armies of the greatest kingdoms in Europe and the Middle East. Alexander ruled an empire that stretched from Greece to India. When he died at 32, his accomplishments and ren_____(2)n were known through_____(3)t the whole world.

Alexander was end_____(4)ed with great strength, intelligence, and pride. He was determined, even as a b_____(5), to _____(6)tdo the accomplishments and expl_____(7)ts of his father, Philip, the shr_____(8)d and p_____(9)erful king of Macedonia. Alexander became king of Macedonia in 336 B.C., when he was only twenty years old. At the time, Greece was in turm_____(10)l. The small city-states into which it was divided were embr_____(11)led in bitter conflicts. In less than four years, Alexander achieved what his father had been unable to accomplish. He conquered Greece and united the Greek cities under the rule of the king of Macedonia. He will always be remembered as a great general and king.

oi as in **oil**

____

____

____

ou as in **ground**

____

____

oy as in **loyal**

____

ow as in **brown**

____

____

____

____

ew as in **grew**

____

Directions The following sentences tell about Alexander the Great. They are not written in the order in which they happened. Number them in the correct sequence, and write them as a paragraph on the lines below.

Definition **Sequence** is the order in which things happen. When you write, it is important to put facts and details in the correct sequence.

___ Four years later, at the age of 18, Alexander led troops into battle and then became an ambassador to Athens, Greece.

___ When he was 14, he began studying under Aristotle, a great teacher and important philosopher.

___ Alexander was born in 356 B.C. in Macedonia.

___ After creating a vast empire stretching from Greece to India, Alexander died of malaria in 323 B.C., at 32 years of age.

___ At the age of 20, Alexander became the king of Macedonia.

___ He was the son of Philip of Macedon, a fearless general, and Olympias, a princess.

Name ____________________

Directions Study the outline. Read each sentence and circle the answer that best completes it. Then write the answer on the line.

Units of Meaning in Words

I. Basic parts of words

- **A.** A base word is a word to which word parts may be added.
  1. The base word of **uncover** is **cover.**
  2. The base word of **unlawful** is **law.**
- **B.** A root is one word part to which other word parts may be added.
  1. The root of **induction** is **duct.**
  2. The root of **important** is **port.**

II. Prefix

- **A.** A prefix is a word part added **in front of** a base word or root.
- **B.** A prefix changes the meaning of a base word or root.
- **C.** Here is an example: **un** is the prefix in **unwrap.**

III. Suffix

- **A.** A suffix is a word part added **in back of** a base word or root.
- **B.** A suffix changes the meaning of a base word or root.
- **C.** Here is an example: **ful** is the suffix in **joyful.**

IV. Prefixes and suffixes

- **A.** They may have only one letter.
- **B.** Here are some examples:
  1. The prefix in **ablaze** is **a.**
  2. The suffix in **indents** is **s.**

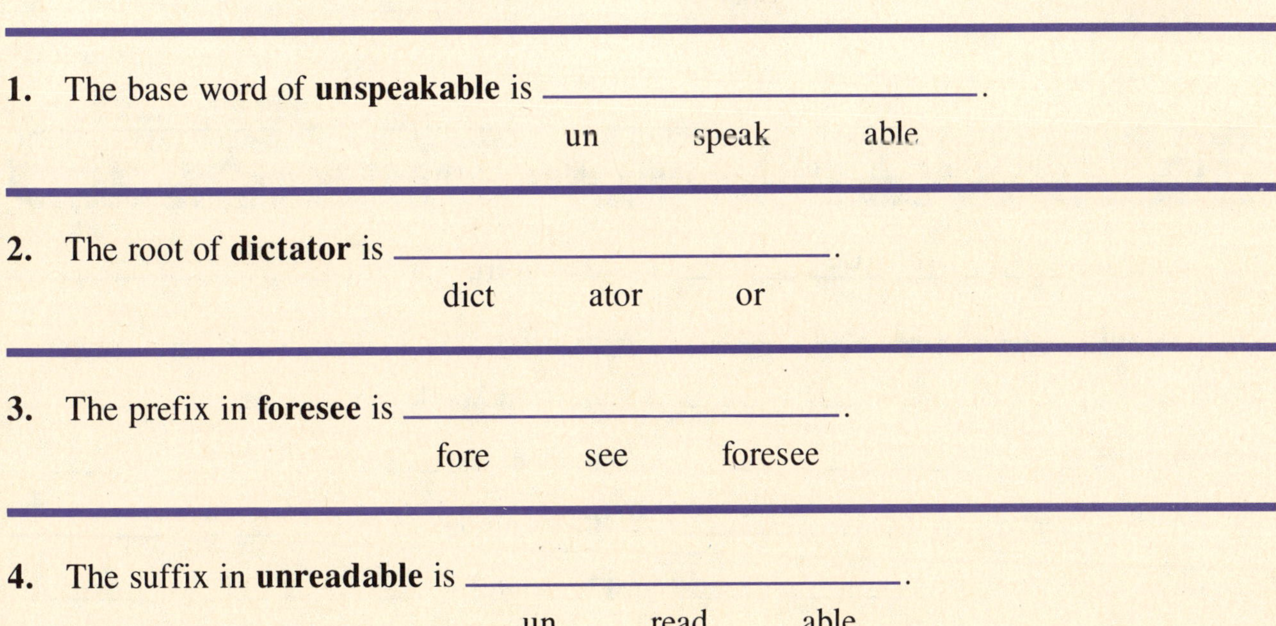

1. The base word of **unspeakable** is ____________________.

un speak able

2. The root of **dictator** is ____________________.

dict ator or

3. The prefix in **foresee** is ____________________.

fore see foresee

4. The suffix in **unreadable** is ____________________.

un read able

Directions Circle the answer that best completes each sentence. Then write it on the line.

1. **Pre** is the prefix of **precooks** and **predicted.** The base word of **precooks** is ______________.
   pre cook s
2. The root of **predicted** is ______________.
   pre dict ed
3. A base word ______________ a word itself.
   is is not
4. A root ______________ **always** a word itself.
   is is not
5. **Mis** is the prefix of **mistake.** The word **mistaken** has ______________ word part(s).
   1 2 3
6. The word **unmistakable** has 4 word parts including ______________ prefixes.
   2 3 4
7. **En** is the prefix of **enlarge.** The word **enlargement** has ______________ word parts.
   2 3 4
8. The word **prepackaged** has ______________ word parts.
   2 3 4

Directions Rewrite each word putting vertical lines between the word parts.

1. enforce en|force	2. untrue ______________
3. forceful ______________	4. misplace ______________
5. forcefully ______________	6. renewable ______________
7. reinforcing ______________	8. entrust ______________
9. reinforcement ______________	10. singing ______________
11. unbeatable ______________	12. rightful ______________
13. inscribe ______________	14. player ______________

Name ______________________________

Rule **Ir**, **im**, **il**, and **in** are prefixes that usually mean *not*.

EXAMPLES

Word	Meaning
irregular	not regular
imperfect	not perfect
illegal	not legal
inexpensive	not expensive

Directions Complete each sentence by choosing a prefix from the box to add to the word below the line. Then write the word on the line.

ir	im	il	in

1. Phil thought the trip to the airport would be an ______________ event.
   significant
2. That night, Phil found it ______________ to avoid dreaming about airplanes.
   possible
3. Phil's dream may have been ______________, but it was exciting.
   rational
4. Although Phil is an ______________ pilot, he was flying a jet in his dream.
   experienced
5. It is highly ______________ for a young boy to be the pilot of a jet.
   regular
6. Since Phil didn't have a license, it was ______________ for him to fly the plane.
   legal
7. All of a sudden, Phil was ______________ of controlling the plane.
   capable
8. Phil felt ______________ because he couldn't read the controls.
   literate
9. It was an ______________ landing, but the plane and passengers were safe.
   perfect

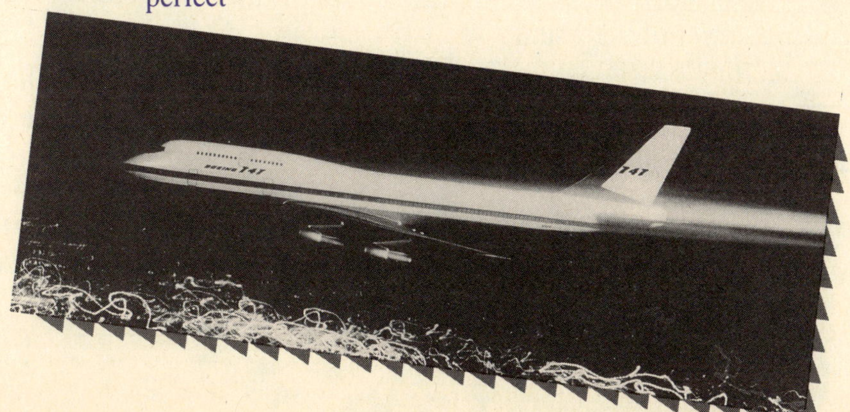

Directions Read the story. Circle each word with a prefix that means **not.**

Michael Faraday

Michael Faraday is known as a great scientist, but the first job he held may have been the same as your first job. He was a news carrier. He worked for low pay and at irregular hours. In the early 1800s, news carriers took their papers from door to door and waited while each client read the newspaper before taking it to the next customer. This was an inexpensive way for people to read the news, but it was inconvenient for news carriers like Michael.

Later, Michael was promoted to bookbinder. Bookbinding taught Michael to work slowly and carefully. He could not be impatient or inexact. As Michael worked, he became curious about the contents of the books. Michael had no schooling, so he was nearly illiterate. Although his reading skills were imperfect, Michael kept practicing. He finally taught himself to read. Michael read every book that came to the bindery. His favorite topic was science. Michael yearned to be a scientist, but that seemed impossible.

One day Michael met Sir Humphry Davy. Sir Davy was astonished at the grasp of science Michael had. He let Michael work as his assistant.

Soon Michael became a full-fledged scientist. He worked to find a way to use electricity as a source of energy. Many other scientists of his time thought his experiments were interesting, but inapplicable to daily life. His experiments proved to be of inestimable value because they eventually led to other inventions, such as the telephone, electric light, TV, and computer.

Directions Find a word you circled that fits each definition.

1. ____________________ not perfect

2. ____________________ not the usual

3. ____________________ not patient

4. ____________________ not suitable to everyday things

5. ____________________ not costing a lot of money

6. ____________________ not able to be estimated or measured

7. ____________________ not able to read

8. ____________________ not handy or easy to do

Name ____

Rule The prefixes **im** and **em** usually mean *in* or *on*. Remember, **im** can also mean *not*.

EXAMPLES

Word	Meaning
immigration	people coming into a country
immeasurable	not measurable
embed	to set something firmly into

Directions Ten words with the prefix **im** or **em** are hidden in the puzzle. Some of the words go across and some go down. Circle each word as you find it in the puzzle. Then write the word beside its meaning.

E R V B S L O T U N I N L
M L X Z B T C I C D M N T
L E B I M M E R S E P O R
I K E M B R O I D E R Y C
M S R P A K B E M B O S S
I M P R O V I S E I P X A
A I M O M I M P U R E E R
J E I B E V I M P O R T B
T A N A N S F G H U Y I Z
L E M B R A C E M I S R W
H E W L I M P E R I L R T
T G X E C Z L N S B C Y G

1. ____________________ to put a decoration or raised design on an article

2. ____________________ to sink into water

3. ____________________ not pure

4. ____________________ to bring in something from another country

5. ____________________ to put in danger

6. ____________________ to hug

7. ____________________ needlework

8. ____________________ not correct or right

9. ____________________ not likely to happen

10. ____________________ to perform something with no preparation

Directions Write a word from the box to complete each sentence.

immature	immigrated	emerged	embark	imagined
employing	improbable	empowered	important	improper
immediately	impatient	improved	embedded	embraced

1. Miguel often ____________________ taking a great vacation with his family.
2. It was ____________________ to Miguel to spend time with his family.
3. Miguel thought the chances of a vacation this year were ____________________.
4. Miguel's father ____________________ from the den one night with a handful of maps.
5. "We are going to ____________________ on a fantastic vacation," Miguel's father said.
6. "____________________ after work tomorrow, we will leave."
7. Miguel was so happy he ____________________ his father.
8. He was ____________________ and wanted to leave right away.
9. He didn't want to act ____________________, so he kept his thoughts to himself.
10. ____________________ in Miguel's mind were his father's words "fantastic vacation."

Directions Now write 3 sentences of your own. In each sentence, include at least one of the **em** or **im** words from the sentences above.

1. ____

____

____

2. ____

____

____

3. ____

____

____

Rule The prefixes **mis** and **mal** usually mean *bad* or *badly*.

EXAMPLES

Word	Meaning
mismatch	bad match
maladjustment	bad adjustment

Directions Circle each word in which **mis** or **mal** is used as a prefix.

1.	mispronounce	**2.**	male	**3.**	misunderstand	**4.**	Maltese
5.	malodorous	**6.**	mislabel	**7.**	malformed	**8.**	misbehave
9.	malnourished	**10.**	misread	**11.**	malpractice	**12.**	maltreat
13.	missile	**14.**	malcontent	**15.**	maladjusted	**16.**	misery
17.	malnutrition	**18.**	misspelling	**19.**	malfunction	**20.**	misquote

Directions Write the word from above that best completes each sentence.

1. People often ignore or ________________ the right methods for caring for dogs.
2. Moving to a new home can cause a dog to become ________________.
3. If you ________________ your dog, it might become aggressive.
4. A ________________ puppy is in danger of sickness and abnormal development.
5. Proper grooming and hygiene should correct any ________________ smells.
6. Daily exercise can prevent a dog from becoming ________________.
7. ________________ is often the cause of poor bone development.
8. Your dog will not ________________ if it has been properly trained.

Directions Use the words in the box to work the crossword puzzle.

misinform	misdeed	malformation	malnutrition
misjoin	misdo	malodorous	misdiagnose
maltreats	mislaid	mistrial	misname

Across

2. to call by a wrong name
5. bad-smelling
6. to decide incorrectly after an examination
7. to give out the wrong information
8. poor nourishment; not enough good food

Down

1. treats badly
3. lost; out of place
4. wrong or unusual formation
5. a trial having no effect in law because some part of it was conducted incorrectly

Name ____

Directions Read the story. Circle each word that begins with the prefix **ir, im, il, in, em, mis,** or **mal.** You will circle fifteen words.

The European Adventurers

In the early 1500s, many adventure-seeking people embarked for the New World from Europe. They faced many troubles at sea. Inaccurate instruments often caused them to misjudge directions. Sometimes, lost at sea for weeks, they were forced to eat things we would consider inedible, such as dry or moldy biscuits. Fierce storms sometimes imperiled their ships. The explorers often faced misfortune with immeasurable courage. Unfortunately, these courageous sailors did a poor job of understanding and preserving the new cultures they discovered.

Sometimes the sailors caused irreparable damage to the way of life of the native people in Central and South America. For example, the Indians were exposed to smallpox, a disease against which they had no immunity. Also, to the great misfortune of the Indians, the sailors destroyed magnificent temples and melted down statues made of gold. They burned books which embodied the history and beliefs of the Mayan Indians. Because of the insensitivity and indifference of the European sailors, these irrecoverable artifacts were destroyed forever. Today it is impossible to regain the rich store of knowledge and art that formed the remarkable Mayan culture.

Directions Read each sentence about the story. If it is correct, write **true.** If it is incorrect, write **false.**

1. Many European adventurers were brave. ____________
2. Life at sea was difficult in the early 1500s. ____________
3. Precise instruments were needed to make navigation easier. ____________
4. All sailors treated the Indians of Central and South America very kindly.

   ____

5. Because of the careful records the exploring sailors kept, we have gained vast knowledge about the Maya.

   ____

Hint Two sentences can often be combined into one sentence for smoother writing by using a connecting word.

EXAMPLES

Word	Meaning
and	also, in addition to, plus
so	as a result
yet	still, but
but	yet, however

Directions Combine a sentence on the left with one on the right by using one of the above connecting words. Write your sentence on the lines below. Remember to use a comma before the connecting word in your new sentence.

1. Almost all the Maya farmed.

2. The Maya did not have wheeled vehicles.

3. The Maya believed that astronomy was important.

4. The houses the Maya built were really square or oval huts.

5. Long ago, Mayan cities teemed with life.

a. They compiled accurate tables of dates on which to expect eclipses of the sun.

b. Many of them also kept hives of stingless bees for honey.

c. Today all that remain are ruins deep in the jungle.

d. They built wide, stone-surfaced roads.

e. The walls were made of poles that were sometimes coated with mud.

Name ____________________

Rule The prefixes **anti** and **counter** mean *against* or *opposite*.

EXAMPLES

Word	Meaning
antipollution	against pollution
counterclockwise	in the opposite direction that the clock runs

Directions Write a word from the box to complete each sentence.

counterbalance	antipollution	counterfeit	antiknock	countermeasure
counterpart	counterclockwise	antilock	antifreeze	countersign

1. My brother joked that he would make ____________________ money to buy a car.
2. Then my dad agreed to ____________________ his loan application.
3. My brother found a car with ____________________ brakes to keep the wheels from locking.
4. Its ____________________ devices limit dangerous exhaust fumes.
5. Gas with ____________________ ingredients will keep the engine from knocking.
6. He turned the wheel ____________________ to check the steering.
7. Weights on the tire rims ____________________ the wheels to keep them from wobbling.
8. As a ____________________ against other tire problems, my brother bought a spare.
9. At home, I helped my brother put ____________________ in his new car.
10. We installed one headlight, but we broke its ____________________.

Directions Write a word from the box to finish each rhyme.

countermove
antifreeze
antibiotic

1. The car engine is cold from the wintery breeze.
   What that engine needs quick is some ______________.
2. Poor Sue is sick. What can she do?
   The doctor may prescribe an ______________ or two.
3. John thought his chess playing did really improve
   Till Jill captured his king in a ______________.

Directions Write the letter of the sentence that answers the question.

____ 1. Which sentence gives a **counterproposal?**
- a. I think our kitchen cabinet top needs to be replaced.
- b. I do not agree with your suggestion, but I have an idea you might like to try.
- c. I think we should buy a new radio.

____ 2. Which sentence expresses **antipathy?**
- a. I hate spiders!
- b. My new roller skates are gone.
- c. Greg prefers hiking off the trails.

____ 3. Which sentence expresses **antisocial** feeling?
- a. Come to my party.
- b. Leave me alone.
- c. Do your homework.

____ 4. Which sentence contains a **countersign?**
- a. Saturday will be sunny and warm.
- b. We have five more months of school.
- c. The password is "cheeseburger."

Name ______________________________

Rule The prefix **de** can mean *down* or *away*.

EXAMPLES

Word	Meaning
descend	go down
deport	send away

Directions Write the correct word from the box on the line beside its definition.

defroster	dejected	delay	detour	departed	descending

1. ______________ a substitute route

2. ______________ to put off or postpone

3. ______________ depressed

4. ______________ a device to remove ice

5. ______________ to have gone away or left

6. ______________ the act of moving down

Directions Write a word from the box to complete each sentence.

1. Our bus ______________ for the football game at 6:00 a.m.

2. The windows were covered with ice because the ______________ was broken.

3. Because of road construction, we were forced to take a ______________.

4. ______________ the steep hill, we hoped the brakes would work.

5. A flat tire caused a two-hour ______________.

6. Even though we missed the game, we were cheerful and not ______________.

Directions Circle each word that contains the prefix **de.**

dean	deodorize	dealt	decimal	deflate	dear
decamp	denounce	dentist	debrief	derailed	decrease
decade	decry	defrost	decode	depth	dehumidifier
departure	denim	deplane	detach	dethrone	detract

Directions Use the words in the box to complete the crossword puzzle.

Across

2. to figure out the meaning of something that is written in secret writing
5. a machine that takes moisture out of the air
6. to get off an airplane
7. to unfasten or disconnect
8. to let air out

Down

1. to take away or cover up the smell of something
3. to take away or make less
4. to remove frost or ice
5. a going away or leaving

Name ______________________________

Rule The prefix **fore** means *front* or *before*. **Post** means *after*.

EXAMPLES

Word	Meaning
forenoon	before noon
postwar	after a war

Directions Circle the word that fits the definition. Then write the word on the line.

1. ______________ to put off until later — postpone / forecast / posterity

2. ______________ to alert to danger beforehand — foreman / forecast / forewarn

3. ______________ first; chief; leading — foremost / postpone / forecast

4. ______________ a thought added after a letter is written — posterity / postpone / postscript

Definition An **analogy** tells the relationship that one thing has to another thing.

EXAMPLES

Water is to **ice** as **bread** is to **toast**.
True is to **false** as **top** is to **bottom**.

Directions Circle the correct ending for each analogy. Then write the answer on the line.

1. **Postpone** is to **delay** as **deliver** is to ______________.
   bring   stop   cancel

2. **Best** is to **worst** as **foremost** is to ______________.
   first   last   next

3. **Predawn** is to **dawn** as **forenoon** is to ______________.
   right   noon   lunch

Directions Choose the word from the box that completes each sentence. Write the letters of the words on the lines.

foremost	posterity	forefinger	foreshadow	forewarned
postgraduate	foretell	forehead	postpone	foresight

1. We hoped the rain on Friday did not __ __ __ __ __ (__) __ __ __ __ a terrible weekend.
2. Not even the meteorologist could __ __ __ __ __ __ (__) __ the weekend weather.
3. We made a group decision not to __ __ __ (__) __ __ __ __ our camping trip.
4. Frank had the __ __ __ __ __ __ (__) __ __ to suggest that we pack our rain gear.
5. Lucas wanted to film our trip for __ __ __ __ (__) __ __ __ __.
6. He filmed a ranger with a bandanna across her __ __ __ __ (__) __ __ __.
7. The ranger __ (__) __ __ __ __ __ __ __ __ us that swimming in the river was dangerous.
8. She told us about the park's __ __ __ __ __ __ (__) __ hiking trails.
9. She pointed to the best trail with her __ __ __ __ __ (__) __ __ __ __.
10. She explained that in __ __ __ __ __ __ __ __ (__) __ __ __ school she had learned about becoming a ranger.

Directions Answer the riddle by writing each circled letter above the number of its sentence.

Riddle Which house weighs the least?

Answer The __ __ __ __ __ __ __ __ __ __!
2 9 4 6 3 1 7 10 8 5

Name ____________________

Directions Read the story. Circle each word that begins with one of the following prefixes: **fore, post, de, counter, anti.**

Antibiotics

An antibiotic is a drug produced by very tiny plants. It helps the body defend itself against dangerous germs. There are many different antibiotics, but penicillin is the foremost one. Antibiotics are called "wonder drugs" because they have caused a decline in so many diseases. For example, bacterial pneumonia and scarlet fever once deprived thousands of people of healthy lives each year. Now these diseases can be treated and cured almost as soon as they are detected. Postoperative infections were once as dangerous as surgery itself. Now these, too, can be cured.

Taking too much of an antibiotic does not help the body. In fact, it makes the antibiotic useless because germs build up a resistance to it. Thus, it is important to take only the amount of antibiotic prescribed by your doctor.

Many doctors forewarn against antibiotics being used too freely—especially in many poor countries where they can be bought without a prescription from a doctor. The power of antibiotics in these countries has greatly decreased. Scientists are forced to devote more and more research to finding new kinds of antibiotics to counteract germs.

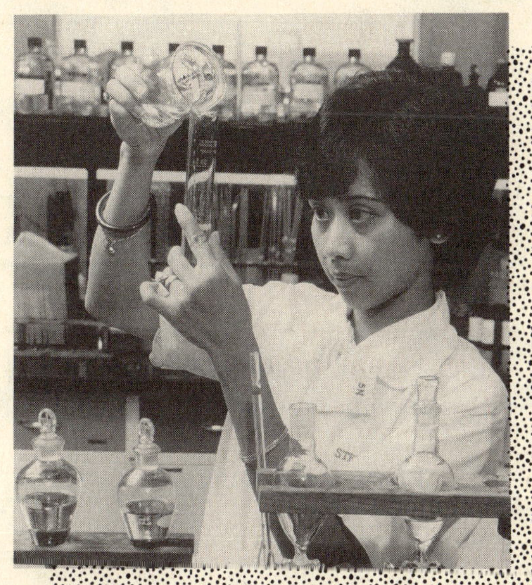

Directions Write a word that you circled that matches each definition.

1. ____________________ a drug that fights germs
2. ____________________ took away
3. ____________________ became less
4. ____________________ guard from harm; keep safe
5. ____________________ to act against or opposite
6. ____________________ first; leading
7. ____________________ warn beforehand
8. ____________________ occurring after a surgical operation

Directions Combine each pair of sentences. Use the word in boldface print as your connecting word. Usually a comma is used before a connecting word, but not before the word **because.**

Hint Two sentences can often be combined into one sentence for smoother writing.

1. Antibiotics are called "wonder drugs." They have a wonderful ability to destroy disease germs quickly. **because**

2. At first, only small amounts of antibiotics could be made. Factories now produce them in huge quantities. **but**

3. Penicillin is the least poisonous antibiotic when it is in contact with body cells. It is probably the most widely used. **and**

Directions Combine each sentence pair below using your own connecting word.

1. Alexander Fleming discovered penicillin in London in 1928. He received the 1945 Nobel Prize in medicine along with two other scientists for its development.

2. The price of 100,000 units of penicillin was once twenty dollars. Today it costs only four cents.

Name ________________________________

Rule The prefix **over** means *too* or *too much*. The prefixes **ultra** and **super** usually mean *very*. **Super** can also mean *over*.

Examples

Word	Meaning
overcrowded	too crowded
ultrafine	very fine
supercold	very cold
supersonic	traveling over the speed of sound

Directions Add the prefix at the top of the column to each word in the column. Write the new word on the line.

1. over		2. ultra		3. super	
time	______	modern	______	market	______
cautious	______	light	______	star	______
confident	______	violet	______	sonic	______
load	______	critical	______	charge	______

Directions Use one of the words you wrote above to complete each of the following sentences.

1. Yukio built a small, homemade ______________ aircraft.
2. He had to work ______________ at his job to pay for the plane.
3. His plane looks old, but it is made of ______________ materials.
4. Compared to ______________ jets, Yukio's plane is very slow.
5. Yukio is careful not to ______________ his small plane.
6. His friends think he is ______________, but Yukio likes to be safe.
7. Yukio wears aviator sunglasses for protection against ______________ rays.

Directions Circle the prefix in each word.

oversleep	supermarket	overdue	ultraloyal
ultrafine	overtime	ultrafashionable	overlong
overjealous	overanxious	ultramodern	superhuman
overemotional	overhasty	oversensitive	ultracritical

Directions Write the word from the box that correctly matches each definition.

1. ______________________ very up-to-date

2. ______________________ too worried

3. ______________________ too emotional

4. ______________________ a large food store

5. ______________________ sleep late

6. ______________________ finding too much fault

7. ______________________ greater than that of a normal person

8. ______________________ extra time beyond regular number of hours of work

9. ______________________ very high fashion

10. ______________________ too much wanting of what others have

11. ______________________ too easily affected by what others say or do

12. ______________________ lengthier than necessary

13. ______________________ very fine

14. ______________________ past due

15. ______________________ very faithful

16. ______________________ moving too fast

Name ______________________________

Rule The prefix **trans** means *across*, *over*, or *beyond*. The prefix **semi** means *half* or *partly*.

EXAMPLES

Word	Meaning
transfer	move from one place to another
transmit	to send across or pass along
semicircle	half a circle
semidark	partly dark

Directions Add the prefix **trans** or **semi** to each base word or root below. The word you make should fit the definition.

1. ______________ **portation:** a means of carrying from one place to another
2. ______________ **mitting:** sending across or passing along
3. ______________ **skilled:** limited in training
4. ______________ **parent:** able to be seen through
5. ______________ **form:** to change the look or condition
6. ______________ **conductor:** a substance used to control current flow
7. ______________ **late:** to change into another form

Directions Write the words you made above to complete the sentences below.

1. Lasers ______________ light into an even more valuable energy source.
2. Lasers use reflective glass and ______________ glass to increase power.
3. The communications and ______________ industries rely on lasers.
4. Lasers are capable of ______________ thousands of telephone calls.
5. ______________ lasers pulse messages through telephone lines.
6. Compact disks use lasers to ______________ computer information into music.
7. In the future, even ______________ workers will use lasers.

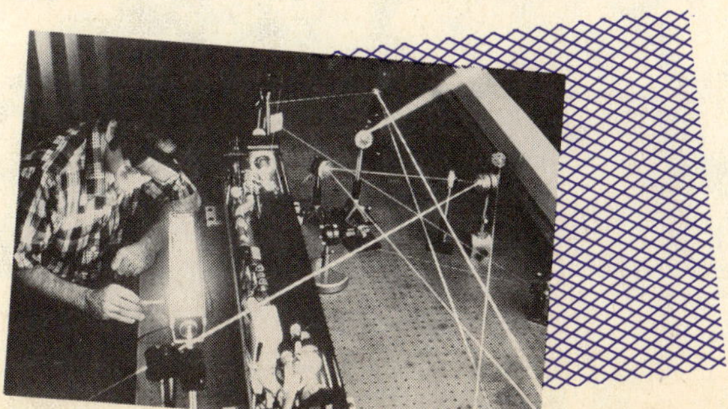

Directions Write the word from the box that correctly completes each sentence.

semidarkness	semicircle	transaction	transient	transferred
Transcontinental	transit	semiskilled	transport	semiannual

1. Stevie, Ray, Uncle Jed, and I sat in a ______________ around the campfire.
2. We were on our ______________ camping trip.
3. In the ______________ of evening, Uncle Jed began his story.
4. To ______________ people across the country, the United States needed a railroad.
5. It was called the ______________ Railroad.
6. The government and two railroad companies made a business ______________.
7. The government ______________ land to the companies as an incentive.
8. The companies hired workers, including immigrants and ______________ people.
9. Most of the workers were unskilled or ______________ laborers.
10. The railroad made ______________ through the Great Plains safer and quicker.

Name ______________________________

Rule The prefix **sub** can mean *under*, *below*, or *not quite*. The prefix **mid** means *the middle part*.

Examples

Words	Meanings
substandard	below the standard
midair	middle of the air

Directions Rewrite each sentence. Use the correct word from the box to replace the phrase in boldface print.

submerge	midday	subfreezing	midnight
midwinter	submarine	subnormal	midway

1. It was **the middle of the day** when the captain received his orders.

2. He changed course and headed his **ship that travels underwater** toward the open sea.

3. He gave the order to **go under water** and left his officers in charge.

4. There were usually **below freezing** temperatures at this time of year.

5. The water was always icy in **the middle of winter.**

6. The temperatures this year, however, were **below normal.**

7. At **twelve o'clock at night,** the captain gave the order to surface.

8. The ship was **halfway** through its journey when it broke through the ice.

Directions Fill in the circle under the word that completes each sentence.

	Sentence			
1.	___ vacations are the best.	Midsummer ❍	Midriff ❍	Midship ❍
2.	My cousin lives on a farm in the ___.	midair ❍	Midwest ❍	midstream ❍
3.	I left my home in the ___ for one month to visit him.	subside ❍	submarine ❍	suburbs ❍
4.	First I rode on the ___ to get to the airport.	midway ❍	subway ❍	subscribe ❍
5.	Before I knew it, I was on a plane in ___.	midair ❍	midtown ❍	suburbs ❍
6.	I tightened the seatbelt against my ___.	subway ❍	midriff ❍	midpoint ❍
7.	Then I read a book with an interesting ___.	midstream ❍	sublet ❍	subplot ❍
8.	I fell asleep ___ through the flight.	midway ❍	sublet ❍	midland ❍
9.	When I got there, a terrible storm had just ___.	subdued ❍	substantial ❍	subsided ❍
10.	The strong winds were now ___.	substandard ❍	subdued ❍	midpoint ❍
11.	A flooded creek had eroded the topsoil, exposing the ___.	midair ❍	midriff ❍	subsoil ❍
12.	At ___, the creek was six feet deep.	midlevel ❍	subfloor ❍	midstream ❍
13.	My cousin's hideout had become a ___ cave.	subterranean ❍	midland ❍	subsoil ❍
14.	Some of the things he kept there were ___ in water.	midair ❍	subway ❍	submerged ❍
15.	At ___, after the clouds were gone, we went outside to look at the stars.	midday ❍	midnight ❍	midriff ❍

Name ____________________

Directions Use the words in the box to answer the questions. Use each word only once.

Rule **Uni, mono, bi,** and **tri** are prefixes that show number. **Uni** and **mono** mean **one. Bi** means **two. Tri** means **three.**

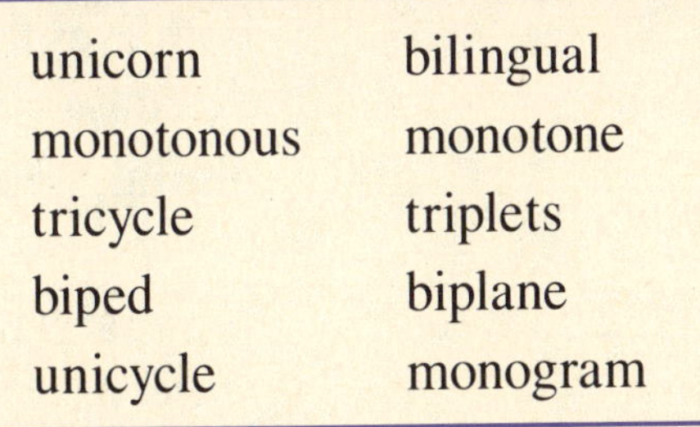

unicorn	bilingual
monotonous	monotone
tricycle	triplets
biped	biplane
unicycle	monogram

1. Which vehicle listed above has three wheels?

____

2. Which word describes people who can speak two languages?

____

3. What is the name of a make-believe horse with one long horn in the center of its forehead?

____

4. How could you describe a boring job in which you do one thing over and over again?

____

5. What is another name for a two-footed animal?

____

6. What are three babies born at the same time to one mother called?

____

7. What is a flat speaking voice that uses just one dull tone called?

____

8. What would you call your initials put together in a design and sewn on your clothes?

____

9. What kind of plane has two sets of wings, one above the other?

____

10. Which vehicle would a clown most likely ride in a circus?

____

Directions Add the prefix **uni, mono, bi,** or **tri** to each base word or root. The word you make should fit the definition.

1. ______________ **pod:** a three-legged support
2. ______________ **forms:** distinctive clothes of a particular group
3. ______________ **son:** speaking the same words at one time
4. ______________ **lingual:** speaking two languages
5. ______________ **noculars:** eyepieces utilizing both eyes to see distant objects
6. ______________ **ennial:** happening every three years
7. ______________ **tonous:** having no variety

Directions Write a word you made above to complete each sentence.

1. Since the folk festival is ______________, Mr. Mulvey takes me every three years.
2. Mr. Mulvey is a photographer, so I help him by carrying his ______________.
3. At first I thought the festival would be ______________, but I was wrong.
4. We took pictures of Russian dancers in colorful ______________.
5. Mr. Mulvey could talk to the Chinese acrobats because he is ______________.
6. A group of Native Americans performed a traditional chant in ______________.
7. The stage was so far away, I had to use ______________.

Name ______________________________

Directions Read the story. Circle each word that begins with one of the following prefixes: **sub, mid, trans, super, over, ultra, uni,** or **bi.** You will circle 13 words.

It is twelve o'clock at night, and you are gazing into the clear, midwinter sky. The midnight stars have transformed the sky into an overwhelming brilliance. The universe beckons overhead as you survey it through your binoculars.

Stars have been a subject of wonder since ancient times. In fact, the study of the stars is rooted in superstition. Long ago, people imagined that the stars were united in groups to show pictures of people, animals, and objects in the sky.

Today, because of ultramodern equipment, astronomers know much more about the night sky. They know that the "star pictures" are not supernatural configurations, but are groups of fixed suns that form constellations in the sky. Satellites, spectrographs, and optical and radio telescopes have helped astronomers measure the distance, motion, and substance of the stars.

Directions Choose a word from those you circled and write it by its definition.

1. ______________ changed
2. ______________ very modern
3. ______________ middle of winter
4. ______________ beyond normal
5. ______________ middle of the night
6. ______________ joined together as one
7. ______________ everything in space
8. ______________ above the head in the sky
9. ______________ something being studied and looked at

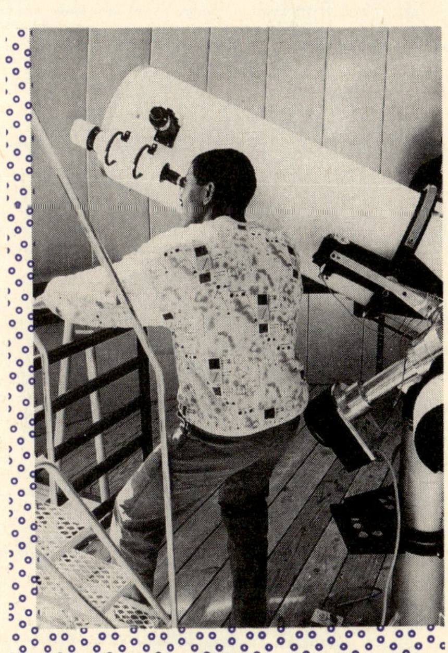

Directions Combine each pair of sentences below into one sentence, using a connecting word such as: **and, so, but, because, yet.** Remember that a comma is usually used before a connecting word, but a comma is not used before the word **because.**

1. The stars are fixed in the sky. If you watch the sky nightly, you will notice that the stars seem to move.

____

____

2. Ancient people believed the earth was the center of the universe. Nicolaus Copernicus proved that the earth moves around the sun.

____

____

3. Until this century, people thought only eight planets orbited the sun. In 1930 Clyde W. Tombaugh discovered Pluto.

____

____

4. It is nearly impossible for astronomers to experiment with the objects they study. They study them from great distances.

____

____

5. Optical telescopes measure the light that comes from stars. Radio telescopes measure radio waves that come from the sky.

____

____

Name ____________________

Definition A **root** is a word part to which prefixes and suffixes can be added to make new words. If you know the meanings of word parts, you can often figure out the meaning of a new word.

Look at these two roots, or word parts, and their meanings.

pos usually means *put* or *place* (**pos**ture)
pel or **pul** usually means *push*, *drive*, or *thrust* (re**pel**)

Directions Read the sentences and underline each word that contains the root **pos, pel,** or **pul.**

1. Jean composed a letter to her friends back home.
2. She wanted to dispel a rumor they had heard.
3. Somehow, word of her expulsion from school had reached them.
4. In fact, the opposite was true.
5. Jean had not been expelled, but was doing very positive things.
6. She felt compelled to let them know the truth.
7. She deposited the letter in the mailbox.

Directions Write the letter of the correct definition next to each word.

____ **1.** deposited		**a.**	that does some good or helps in some way
____ **2.** expelled		**b.**	the act of forcing out
____ **3.** composed		**c.**	placed for safekeeping
____ **4.** dispel		**d.**	made to do something
____ **5.** expulsion		**e.**	created or wrote
____ **6.** positive		**f.**	the other side, something very different from
____ **7.** opposite		**g.**	driven out, forced out
____ **8.** compelled		**h.**	to make disappear

Rule The root **port** means *carry*. The root **ject** means *throw*.

EXAMPLES

Word	Meaning
de**port**	to force to leave
e**ject**	to throw out

Directions Complete each sentence with a word from the box.

rejected	portable	imported	reports
important	eject	report	deportment

1. Carlos has an extremely ________________ job at the electronics factory.
2. He inspects each piece of equipment, determining whether each will be sold or ________________.
3. Carlos begins his inspections by checking the ________________ televisions.
4. Carlos ________________ his inspections to the video department.
5. He evaluates not only the video recorders, but the mechanisms that allow them to ________________ a tape that has been viewed.
6. He also checks the various parts that have been ________________ from other countries.
7. When Carlos completes his inspections, he writes a detailed ________________ for his supervisor, Bob.
8. Bob has always been impressed with Carlos's excellent work and his fine ________________.

Directions Match each word with its definition.

____	**1.** reject	**a.**	to throw; to force out
____	**2.** deportment	**b.**	conduct; behavior
____	**3.** portable	**c.**	to refuse; to discard
____	**4.** report	**d.**	a statement or account of
____	**5.** export	**e.**	to send goods to another country for sale
____	**6.** eject	**f.**	able to be carried easily

Name ____

Rule The root **dict** usually means *tell* or *say*. The root **aud** means *hear*.

EXAMPLES

Word	Meaning
dictate	to say with authority
audible	loud enough to be heard

Directions Read the sentences and underline each word that contains the root **aud** or **dict.**

1. The crew is working to create the audio portion of a commercial.
2. Abby, who will perform the voice-over, speaks with crisp diction.
3. At the audition, the commercial's director was impressed with her.
4. He knew Abby's pleasant voice would appeal to an audience.
5. Abby looked in her pocket dictionary for a word's pronunciation.
6. The director issued an edict to Abby and the crew: "Begin recording!"
7. When he played back the recording, it was barely audible.
8. "I predict we will find that something is wrong with our equipment," he said.

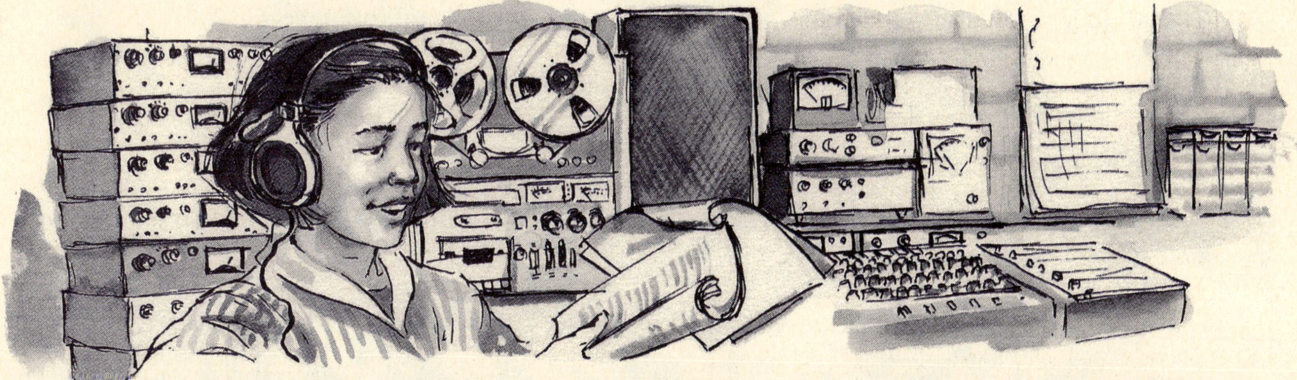

Directions Match each word with its definition.

____ **1.** audio		**a.**	a strong statement or command
____ **2.** dictate		**b.**	a group of people who listen or watch
____ **3.** edict		**c.**	sound
____ **4.** audible		**d.**	a book containing definitions for words
____ **5.** contradict		**e.**	to say firmly; to give an order
____ **6.** dictionary		**f.**	to forecast; to say ahead of time
____ **7.** predict		**g.**	able to be heard
____ **8.** audience		**h.**	to deny; to say the opposite of

Directions Complete each sentence with a word from the box.

Rule The roots **cap, cept,** or **ceipt** mean *take* or *seize.* (**cap**ture)

capable	reception	accept	capacity	captured
capitol	acceptance	receipts	receptacle	captivating

1. Last night, we attended an elegant ______________.
2. The huge room was filled to ______________.
3. Carol gave a speech to ______________ the nomination for governor.
4. Everyone knows she is ______________ of being a great governor.
5. An excellent speaker, Carol ______________ the crowd's attention.
6. It was an especially ______________ speech.
7. She asked that written suggestions be placed in a ______________.
8. She offered ______________ to those who made contributions.
9. Today, the newspapers praised Carol's ______________ speech.
10. If she wins the election, she will move to the state ______________.

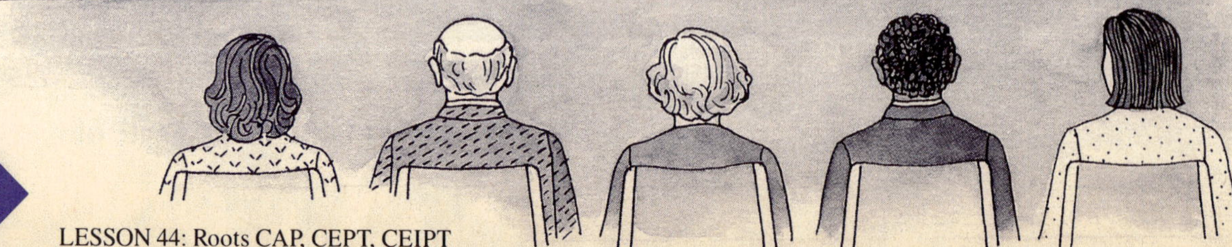

Name ____________________

Rule The roots **spec** and **spect** mean *see, look,* or *examine*. The roots **mit** and **miss** mean *send* or *let go*.

EXAMPLES

Word	Meaning
spectator	an onlooker
dis**miss**	to send away

Directions Ten words containing the roots **spec** or **spect, mit** or **miss** are hidden in the puzzle. Some of the words go across and some go down. Circle each word and write it on the line.

S	T	Q	A	D	M	I	T	I	R	S	P
U	P	E	B	N	K	N	I	U	P	F	E
B	P	H	S	I	N	S	P	E	C	T	R
M	A	S	R	C	H	P	B	D	Q	G	S
I	K	X	E	M	V	E	W	O	J	T	P
T	R	M	S	P	E	C	I	M	E	N	E
F	E	B	P	H	J	T	E	V	C	X	C
U	M	O	E	G	Z	O	M	I	T	V	T
Z	I	G	C	O	A	R	W	D	I	L	I
G	T	Y	T	A	W	R	V	F	J	D	V
Y	T	Y	R	N	L	C	K	N	Q	Y	E
D	I	S	M	I	S	S	A	L	M	Z	E

1. ____________________
2. ____________________
3. ____________________
4. ____________________
5. ____________________
6. ____________________
7. ____________________
8. ____________________
9. ____________________
10. ____________________

Directions Complete each sentence with a word from the puzzle.

1. I ____________________ that I was squeamish about the blood test at first.
2. From my ____________________, it wasn't really fun.
3. I certainly ____________________ the nurse who drew the blood.
4. She said she would ____________________ the sample to the lab.
5. There, the ____________________ will be evaluated.

Rule The root **man** means *hand.*

EXAMPLES

Word	**Meaning**
manual	made or done by hand

Directions Read each sentence and underline the word that has the root **man.**

1. My older brother, David, is the manager of Zippy's Video Arcade.
2. David has been managing the arcade for nearly two years.
3. Since he manipulates the controls quickly, David can win any video game he plays.
4. Some of the games are voice-activated, but I prefer those that are manual.
5. If I use my best manners, I can usually convince David to play a game with me.
6. We play Blast-Off, a game that allows us to maneuver astronauts on the screen.
7. The game's object is to keep an astronaut from being placed in manacles by an alien.
8. I am working on the manuscript for a book of tips about winning the game.

Directions Write the letter of the correct word beside its definition.

____ **1.** polite way of behaving	**a.** manipulate
____ **2.** handcuffs; objects to tie the hands together	**b.** manuscript
____ **3.** worked by hand, as a car transmission	**c.** manners
____ **4.** something written by hand	**d.** manacles
____ **5.** fingernail and hand care	**e.** manicure
____ **6.** to have charge or direct	**f.** manage
____ **7.** to move around skillfully by hand	**g.** manual

Name ______________________________

Directions Read the story. Use a word from the box to complete each unfinished sentence.

positive	dictionary	deceive	manuscripts	adjective
report	admit	portfolio	prospector	subject

I have always wanted to be a writer. I carry a pocket ______ (1) around with me so I can look up new and interesting words. Sometimes you need a good ______ (2), like horrendous or cunning, to describe a noun. I like to write about almost any ______ (3), ranging from animals to space travel.

I have a ______ (4) of my work that I carry around. It has all my ______ (5). One of the best is a story about a ______ (6) who is looking for gold in the 1800s. He is ______ (7) he has found a big strike. But it turns out that the ______ (8) of the gold is false. Someone had hidden the fake gold to ______ (9) him. Of course, the story is fiction because I must ______ (10) I don't know if it really happened.

Directions Read the paragraph. Underline the sentence that is the main idea. Then write the sentences that give supporting details. Draw a line through the sentence that does not give a supporting detail.

Hint When you write a paragraph, all the information in it should tell about the same thing. One sentence should state the main idea. The other sentences should give supporting details.

Before I could play baseball, I had to submit to a complete physical checkup at the doctor's office. She checked my heart with a portable machine and inspected my ears and eyes. There were many magazines for people to read in the waiting room. The nurse gave me an injection for my hay fever. The doctor did not omit her lecture about eating well. When she dismissed me, the doctor predicted that I would be capable of having a good season as pitcher.

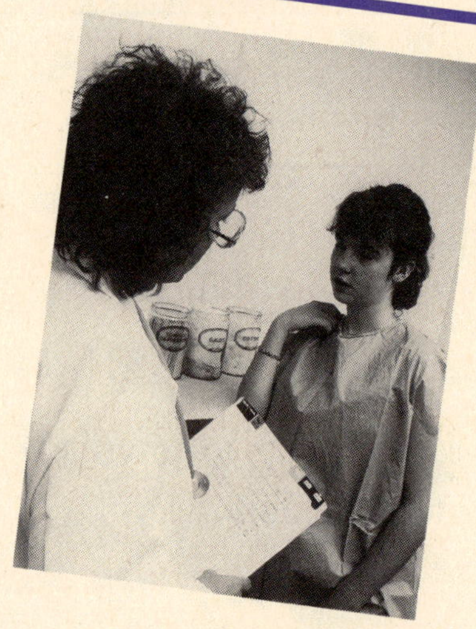

Directions Now go back through the paragraph and circle each word that has a root that you have studied in this unit. Write the words on the lines.

Name ____________________

Definition A **compound word** is made up of two or more other words. Each word word can stand on its own and still have meaning.

EXAMPLES

matchbox = match + box
rattlesnake = rattle + snake

Directions Read the sentences and underline each compound word. Be sure that each word you underline is made up of two words that can stand on their own.

1. My grandparents live next to a famous lighthouse at the ocean.
2. Each year, for my birthday, we have a celebration at their house.
3. Since my birthday occurs in the summertime, we play outdoor games.
4. My sisters like to play baseball, but I prefer volleyball.
5. My grandfather and my mother, who is in a wheelchair, play chess outside.
6. They lean over the chessboard with great concentration.
7. Dad usually plays horseshoes with my grandmother.
8. My sisters and I climb up to the treehouse, which we built two years ago.
9. After sunset, we use a flashlight to try to signal the lighthouse.
10. Then, dressed in warm sweatshirts, we eat cupcakes and drink milk.

Directions Choose the correct compound word from those you underlined and write it on the line beside its definition.

1. older family members ____________________
2. a portable electric light ____________________
3. small cakes ____________________
4. a chair mounted on wheels ____________________
5. heavy cotton shirts ____________________

Directions Choose a word from the box and write it on the line in front of the correct word to make a compound word.

water	thunder	row	hot	snow	air
pine	rain	box	hail	beef	steam

1. ________ boat 2. ________ car 3. ________ steak

4. ________ flakes 5. ________ cakes 6. ________ storm

7. ________ apple 8. ________ stones 9. ________ melon

10. ________ drops 11. ________ ship 12. ________ plane

Directions Write each compound word you made under the correct heading.

Kinds of food

1. ________
2. ________
3. ________
4. ________

Kinds of vehicles

1. ________
2. ________
3. ________
4. ________

Kinds of weather

1. ________ 2. ________

3. ________ 4. ________

Name ______________________

Rule The possessive form is used to show that a person or an animal owns, has, or possesses something. To make a singular word show possession, usually add an apostrophe and an s (**'s**). If a word is plural and ends in s, just add an apostrophe.

EXAMPLES

Mike's boat
the **dog's** feet
the **sun's** rays
girls' uniforms

Directions Read each group of words. If the words show that only one person or animal has something, write **one** on the first line. If the words show that more than one person or animal has something, write **more than one.** Then on the second line write the possessive form that can stand for each phrase.

1. the coat of Blair ______ ______
2. the snout of the seal ______ ______
3. the market of the farmers ______ ______
4. the owners of the dogs ______ ______
5. the nest of the owls ______ ______
6. the locker room of the boys ______ ______
7. the scores of the bowlers ______ ______
8. the skin of the snake ______ ______
9. thc skateboard of Ellen ______ ______
10. the home of the zebras ______ ______
11. the kitchen of Mom ______ ______
12. the home of the muskrat ______ ______

Rule To make a word show possession: **1.** add **'s** to a singular or a plural word not ending in s, **2.** add an apostrophe (') to a plural word ending in s.

EXAMPLES

Bill's house
the **children's** books
James's portfolio
the **bears'** home

Directions Read each sentence. Write the correct possessive form of the word at the right.

1. Our ________________ curriculum includes computer skills. (school)
2. It is our ________________ turn to use the computer room today. (class)
3. Ms. ________________ class used the special room yesterday. (Kinkaid)
4. All the ________________ computer manuals must be distributed. (students)
5. Mr. ________________ computer is at the front of the class. (Moss)
6. As he turns it on, the ________________ green screen lights up. (computer)
7. Then, the screens light up on each ________________ computer. (student)
8. I hear the sound of ________________ fingers on the keyboard. (Kevin)
9. ________________ word-processing skills are excellent. (Chris)
10. The other ________________ skills are not quite as advanced. (sixth-graders)
11. After school, Tomás and I practice on his ________________ computer. (family)
12. We are welcome to use any of his ________________ software. (parents)
13. With ________________ help, my abilities are improving. (Tomás)

Name ______________________________

Definition A **contraction** is a short way to write two words. The two words are written together, but one or more letters are left out. An apostrophe is used in place of the missing letters.

EXAMPLES

is not = isn't

The letter **o** has been left out.

you have = you've

The letters **ha** have been left out.

Directions Write a contraction from the box to complete each sentence. Then, on the lines at the right, write the two words that form each contraction.

you'd	she's	don't	You're	shouldn't
you'll	won't	she'd	Jerry's	I'm

1. Don, I wish ______________ join my committee for the dance. ______________
2. Barb originally said ______________ help me in planning. ______________
3. Since ______________ busy with decorations, she backed out. ______________
4. I'm sure ______________ be a real asset in planning! ______________
5. ______________ busy with the refreshment committee. ______________
6. Otherwise, ______________ certain he would help us. ______________
7. Tonight's meeting ______________ take too much time. ______________
8. It ______________ take more than an hour. ______________
9. ______________ not going to be sorry you've agreed to help! ______________
10. You ______________ know how happy you've made me! ______________

Directions In the first column, write the two words the contraction stands for. In the second column, write the letter or letters that were left out.

		Words	Letter or Letters Left Out
1.	aren't	__________	__________
2.	Lee's	__________	__________
3.	won't	__________	__________
4.	they're	__________	__________
5.	where's	__________	__________
6.	she'll	__________	__________
7.	we've	__________	__________
8.	I'm	__________	__________
9.	you'd	__________	__________
10.	it's	__________	__________

Directions Underline the contraction in each sentence. Then write the two words it stands for.

1. Where's the movie section of the newspaper? __________
2. Do you think that'll be enough money for the movie? __________
3. I hope we're not too late to make it to the matinee. __________
4. The movies at the East Cinema don't always start on time. __________
5. We'd better hurry if we want to see this show! __________

Name ____________________

Remember these rules for dividing words into syllables.

When a word has a prefix, divide the word between the prefix and the base word or the root. Some prefixes have more than one syllable.

When a word has a suffix, divide the word between the suffix and the base word or the root. Some suffixes have more than one syllable.

Sometimes a word has a prefix and a suffix with the base word or the root. If each word part has a vowel part, then each part is a syllable.

Divide a compound word between the words that make up the compound word. Then divide the smaller words into syllables if necessary.

Directions Write the number of vowel sounds you hear in each word. Then divide the word into syllables using vertical lines.

1. compel ___ ____________
2. wallpaper ___ ____________
3. propose ___ ____________
4. audible ___ ____________
5. icebreaker ___ ____________
6. yearbook ___ ____________
7. capable ___ ____________
8. accept ___ ____________
9. submit ___ ____________
10. inspector ___ ____________
11. dictation ___ ____________
12. posture ___ ____________
13. barefoot ___ ____________
14. admit ___ ____________
15. propulsion ___ ____________
16. battleship ___ ____________
17. deceiving ___ ____________
18. dismissal ___ ____________
19. audition ___ ____________
20. ringmaster ___ ____________
21. collarbone ___ ____________
22. oppose ___ ____________
23. dictionary ___ ____________
24. propellant ___ ____________

Directions Read each sentence. Underline each two-syllable word. Circle each three-syllable word. Draw a box around each four-syllable word. Then use vertical lines to divide each word you marked into syllables in the correct column.

1. Our girls' basketball team made it to the championship tournament.
2. The team has played excellently during the winter season.
3. Playing forward, Beth achieved an impressive record.
4. Beth is tall and dedicated, and she shoots accurately.
5. The team's co-captains, Sue and Jo, have been outstanding this year.
6. Each game attracted numerous cheering spectators.
7. Last night's game was incredibly exciting.
8. Beth executed some complicated moves.
9. The game was especially filled with suspense.
10. The score was surprisingly close.

Two-Syllable	Three-Syllable	Four-Syllable

Name ______________________________

Directions Use the words in the box to complete the sentences.

downstairs	neighbor's	newspaper	Where's	bedroom
couldn't	homemade	he'd	bookcase	dog's

1. Even though ____________ eaten earlier, Tod was hungry when he went to bed.
2. He crept ____________ to see if there was any ____________ blueberry pie left.

---

1. My ____________ voice could wake the dead.
2. Every evening we can hear him as he bellows, "____________ the ____________?"

---

1. Ronnie ____________ find his ____________ leash.
2. He looked in his ____________ and under the ____________.

Directions Choose one of the sentence pairs above. Write the main idea on the first line. Write the supporting detail on the second line. Now write two more sentences yourself to make a paragraph. Be sure your sentences support, or give more information about, the main idea. Include one contraction, one possessive, and one compound word in your sentences.

____

____

____

____

____

____

____

____

____

____

____

Directions The following sentences are a mixed-up paragraph. Write them on the lines in the correct order to make a paragraph, with the main idea sentence first. Circle each contraction, possessive, and compound word. Then write them on the lines below.

This means she's able to tell about someone's personality by looking at the person's writing. Carla is a handwriting expert. She once proved her ability by helping the police find a missing person. She claims that when all is said and done, it's a better identity test than using fingerprints.

Contractions: ____________________

Possessives: ____________________

Compound words: ____________________

Name ______________________________

Rule The suffixes **er** or **or** mean something or someone who does something. They can change a verb into a noun.

EXAMPLES

edit	edit**or**
mix	mix**er**

Rule The suffix **ist** also means someone who does something. But it changes one kind of noun into another kind of noun.

EXAMPLES

archaeology	archaeolog**ist**
optometry	optometr**ist**

Directions Write the word that goes with each meaning. Circle the words you do not use.

photographer	optometrist	geologist	stretcher
juror	machinist	computer	farmer
customer	generator	organist	geology
machinery	collector	creator	organism

1. one who grows crops ______________

2. one who studies rocks ______________

3. one who takes pictures ______________

4. something that produces electricity ______________

5. something that works quickly with numbers and facts ______________

6. one who serves on a jury ______________

7. one who plays a musical instrument ______________

8. one who shops for goods ______________

9. one who works with machines ______________

10. one who makes something ______________

11. something that can be used to carry a person ______________

12. one who gathers large numbers of similar items ______________

13. one who tests vision and prescribes glasses ______________

Directions There are words hidden in the puzzle that have the suffixes **er, or,** or **ist.** Some of the words go across, and some go down. Circle each word as you find it, and write it in the correct column.

D	I	V	E	R	J	G	A	B	J	C	T
M	K	I	R	E	A	L	I	S	T	G	Y
I	R	S	T	A	U	R	T	V	K	A	P
N	B	I	M	L	B	B	A	R	C	R	I
E	C	T	N	I	B	C	U	B	R	C	S
R	T	O	U	R	I	S	T	M	T	O	T
L	S	R	T	R	A	I	N	E	R	M	B
A	R	T	I	S	T	P	S	E	B	P	A
O	E	A	C	T	O	R	T	R	C	U	T
D	O	C	T	O	R	W	Y	H	G	T	T
E	S	C	A	L	A	T	O	R	U	E	E
C	D	G	F	E	S	K	A	T	E	R	R

er	**or**	**ist**
______________	______________	______________
______________	______________	______________
______________	______________	______________
______________	______________	______________
______________		
______________		

Directions Now write the correct word from the puzzle beside its definition.

1. a moving stairway that carries people up or down ______________
2. one who travels ______________
3. one who teaches animals to do tricks ______________

Name ____________________

Rule The suffix **er** is used to compare two objects or people. The suffix **est** is used to compare more than two objects or people.

EXAMPLES

February is **cold**, but January was **colder**.
Kim is **taller** than Jo, but Peg is the **tallest** of all.

Directions Add **er** or **est** to the base word you see below the line. Remember that when the base word ends in **e,** drop the **e** before adding **er** or **est.** If the base word ends in **y,** change the **y** to **i** before adding **er** or **est.**

1. *Laugh It Up* is by far the ____________ book I ever read.
(great)

2. Willie is the book's hero, and he is the ____________ character in it.
(silly)

3. He is surely ____________ than the character Anna, who never smiles.
(funny)

4. In the story, Anna is several years ____________ than Willie.
(young)

5. Despite her youth, Anna is the ____________ character in the book.
(weary)

6. Willie decides to make Anna the ____________ person in the world.
(happy)

7. He devises funny stunts to make her ____________ than she's ever been.
(happy)

8. Each of Willie's stunts is ____________ than the last!
(tricky)

9. Finally, Anna smiles the ____________ grin Willie has ever seen.
(wide)

Directions Look at the base word in boldface print. Then read each short paragraph. Use the base word or a comparative of the word with **er** or **est** to complete each unfinished sentence. You may use the base word and two comparatives in a paragraph. You may also use a word twice.

1. **busy**

The ________________ highway was the scene of many traffic jams. The ________________ corner was Randle and Foote streets. Even on Sundays this corner is ________________ than any other.

2. **bright**

That star is the ________________ one in the sky. It is ________________ than the one close to it, which is also a very ________________ star.

3. **wet**

George gets ________________ in a rainstorm than anyone I know. He doesn't carry an umbrella. He says he's afraid it will get ________________.

4. **happy**

Hannah always seems to be ________________. She is ________________ than her brother Hal. I wonder what she's so ________________ about.

5. **high**

Connie can jump ________________ than Alice. She can jump the ________________ of anyone on the track team. Everyone on the team can jump ________________ than I can.

6. **long**

The new trail to the top of the mountain was ________________. Maybe it seemed ________________ than the old one because we were so hungry. It really seemed like the ________________ trail we had ever hiked.

Name ______________________________

Hint The suffixes **ous** and **al** can change a noun into an adjective.

EXAMPLES

Suffix	Meaning	Word
ous	full of, having, like	courage—courage**ous**
al	like, having to do with	comic—comic**al**

Directions Read each sentence and look at the word below the line. Form an adjective using one of the suffixes above. If the base word ends in **y,** change the **y** to **i** before adding **ous.** If it ends in **f,** usually change the **f** to **v** before adding **ous.**

1. The house at the end of the block is a ______________ monument.
   (historic)
2. Miriam conducts ______________ tours through the house.
   (education)
3. She leads her tour groups through its ______________ rooms.
   (glory)
4. Miriam points out the ______________ woodwork in the house.
   (ornament)
5. She explains how the ______________ furniture was created.
   (tradition)
6. Miriam discusses the lives of the home's ______________ owners.
   (colony)
7. She shares many ______________ stories with her groups.
   (humor)
8. Some of the owners' antics were really quite ______________.
   (comic)
9. Of course, life during colonial times could be ______________.
   (danger)
10. When Miriam feels ______________, she says the house is haunted.
    (mischief)

Directions Read the words in the box. Then use the clues at the bottom to complete the crossword puzzle.

sentimental	poisonous	mysterious	ornamental	fallacious
nervous	national	natural	famous	mountainous

Across

1. having to do with a country
6. full of mystery
7. having a reputation; being well-known
8. full of feeling
9. mistaken

Down

1. being tense
2. having to do with nature
3. full of harmful substances
4. having many mountains
5. for decoration

Name ______________________________

Rule The suffix **ward** can change a noun into an adjective or adverb. The suffix **en** can change a noun into a verb or an adjective. The suffix **ize** can change a noun into a verb.

EXAMPLES

Suffix	Meaning	Word
ward	in the direction of, toward	home**ward**
en	to make, to become, made of	wood**en**
ize	to make, to become	legal**ize**

Directions Read the sentences and underline each word with the suffix **ward, en,** or **ize.** Then write each word you underlined in the correct column.

1. I did not realize that going out in the boat would frighten you.
2. I apologize for assuming that you would want to go seaward with us.
3. You can watch from the shore as we loosen the ropes and go forward.
4. Before we get into the boat, we always make sure to fasten our life jackets.
5. Gregory kicks off from the shore with a backward push.
6. I look skyward to make sure the weather is good.
7. When we are on the boat, we all like to sing and harmonize loudly.
8. We like to modernize old songs.
9. When the days begin to shorten, we don't stay in the boat very long.

en	ward	ize
______	______	______
______	______	______
______	______	______
______	______	______

Directions Complete each sentence by adding **ward, en,** or **ize** to each base word below the line.

1. This delay on the ground will certainly ______ (length) our travel time.

2. I had hoped that the clear skies and strong wind would ______ (short) it.

3. Does it ______ (sad) you to wait motionless on the ground for so long?

4. It was nice of the pilot to ______ (apology) for the long delay.

5. The flight attendant asks us to look ______ (for) as he demonstrates safety procedures.

6. Make sure Danny is not looking ______ (back) during the demonstration.

7. The flight attendants ______ (standard) the information they present.

8. The airplane finally begins to taxi down the runway and move ______ (sky).

9. Its gleaming silver nose points ______ (up).

10. As we soar into the sky, my spirits begin to ______ (light).

11. Now I can ______ (real) my dream of a vacation.

12. Danny and I look ______ (down) at the landscape.

13. Hardly a word is ______ (spoke) as we gaze at the scenery below.

Name ______________________________

Rule When the suffix **ful** is added to an noun, it changes the word either into an adjective or into a different noun. The suffix **ness** changes adjectives into nouns.

EXAMPLES

Suffix	Meaning	Word
ful	full of, having a tendency to be	dread**ful** care**ful**
ful	a certain amount	bucket**ful** arm**ful**
ness	quality, condition of being	dark**ness** sweet**ness**

Directions Complete each sentence by adding **ful** or **ness** to each base word below the line.

1. Marta is a hairdresser with very ________ (skill) hands.
2. She is always serious and ________ (care) about her work.
3. Without such skill, the results can be ________ (dread)!
4. My hair is hard to manage because of its ________ (thick).
5. I am ________ (hope) that Marta can tame this wild mane!
6. Marta fills me with ________ (glad) when she cuts my hair.
7. She is always ________ (truth) when offering styling tips.
8. I am ________ (thank) to have her as my hairdresser.

Directions There are words containing the suffixes **ful** or **ness** hidden in the puzzle. Some of the words go across and some go down. Circle each word as you find it, and write it in the correct column.

ful

____

____

____

____

____

____

ness

____

____

____

____

____

____

B	C	F	G	H	J	B	L	D	R	S	D
H	A	R	M	F	U	L	A	X	Y	T	A
S	R	B	N	G	C	A	F	Y	Z	R	M
Z	E	A	S	N	D	C	D	P	Q	I	P
P	F	G	T	M	X	K	L	M	R	C	N
W	U	F	N	E	W	N	E	S	S	T	E
G	L	U	D	F	G	E	H	K	M	N	S
T	D	L	P	H	T	S	N	I	T	E	S
F	I	T	N	E	S	S	O	L	V	S	T
T	F	O	C	R	Z	P	R	L	W	S	L
Q	J	B	F	P	A	I	L	F	U	L	B
B	H	E	A	L	T	H	F	U	L	D	C
D	A	R	K	N	E	S	S	L	M	N	P

Directions Write a word from the puzzle to complete each sentence.

1. Jack is very ______________________ about maintaining his good health.
2. He exercises every day to improve his physical ______________________.
3. Jack always eats ______________________ food so his body will be strong.
4. He would never do anything that would be ______________________ to his body.

Name ______________________________

Directions Each word in the box has a suffix you studied in this unit. Read the editorial and write the word from the box that completes each sentence. The suffix below each line will help you choose the correct word. You will not use all the words in the box.

additional	sideward	brightness	agonize	mechanical	dangerous	peaceful
generalize	arsonists	forward	furious	greatness	organists	numerous
fighters	drivers	frightful	stiffen	shorten	inspector	creator

Our town has seen some ______________ (1 ful) events during the last weeks. ______________ (2 ist) have burned down ______________ (3 ous) buildings. We must ______________ (4 en) the punishment for this kind of crime. Arson is both ______________ (5 ous) to people and a threat to business. As an ______________ (6 al) worry, the chief fire ______________ (7 or) says it is also a danger to the fire______________ (8 er) whose job it is to put out the fires.

As a city, we must not be discouraged by the ______________ (9 ness) of the problem. We must move ______________ (10 ward) to solve it. Meanwhile, we ______________ (11 ize) for anyone who has lost a home or business.

Directions Read the statements. Put a check in front of each statement that is a paraphrase of the editorial. Put an X in front of each one that is not a paraphrase of what the editorial says.

____ **1.** Arson is a terrible crime.

____ **2.** Arsonists should live somewhere out of the city.

____ **3.** Firefighters should have safer equipment.

____ **4.** The penalty for arson should be increased.

____ **5.** The city should move to fight arson.

____ **6.** The chief inspector should be replaced.

Directions Think about the things you read, see, or hear during any one week. Many of these things try to persuade, or convince you to think or act a certain way. Read the examples below. Circle each one that is written to convince or persuade. Draw a line through each one that is not.

1. an advertisement for soap that tells you people will love you if you use it
2. a funny TV comedy show
3. an editorial that calls for citizens to vote in the next election
4. a news story about an event in China
5. a radio program that plays music
6. a letter from a cousin asking you to come and visit
7. a poster that tries to get people to join the army
8. a set of directions telling how to make a model plane

Directions Write three or more sentences to convince someone to act or think in a certain way. You may write an editorial for the school paper or an advertisement for something you want to sell. Use at least five words that have the following suffixes.

er	or	ist	er	est	ous	al	ward	en	ize	ful	ness

Name ______________________________

Rule The suffixes **hood**, **ship**, and **ment** can change one noun into another noun.

EXAMPLES

Suffix	Meaning	Word
hood	state or condition of being	mother**hood**
ship	state, rank of, art of something	governor**ship**
ment	act of, state of something	improve**ment**

Directions Fill in the circle under the word that correctly completes each sentence.

1.	Sara and Joan share a special ____.	friendship ❍	courtship ❍	falsehood ❍
2.	They grew up in the same ____.	motherhood ❍	authorship ❍	neighborhood ❍
3.	They tell stories about their ____.	enrollment ❍	childhood ❍	likelihood ❍
4.	They recall one story with great ____.	authorship ❍	enjoyment ❍	adulthood ❍
5.	The girls had a shared ____—measles.	friendship ❍	ailment ❍	kinship ❍
6.	Suffering through it was a ____.	falsehood ❍	placement ❍	hardship ❍
7.	The experience created a special ____.	governorship ❍	kinship ❍	statement ❍
8.	Sara has never had an ____ with Joan.	argument ❍	partnership ❍	management ❍
9.	Joan has never told Sara a ____.	brotherhood ❍	falsehood ❍	astonishment ❍
10.	Many people view the girls with ____.	amendment ❍	childhood ❍	astonishment ❍
11.	They marvel at this incredible ____.	livelihood ❍	partnership ❍	craftsmanship ❍
12.	Some even envy the girls' ____.	ailment ❍	improvement ❍	relationship ❍
13.	The girls will be friends through ____.	adulthood ❍	scholarship ❍	statehood ❍
14.	They have a ____ to each other.	commitment ❍	womanhood ❍	championship ❍

Directions Circle the word that correctly completes each analogy. Then write the word on the line.

Definition An **analogy** tells the relationship one thing has to another. This is an analogy: **Light** is to **dark** as **slow** is to **fast.** (**Light** is the opposite of **dark** as **slow** is the opposite of **fast.**)

1. **Up** is to **down** as **truth** is to ______________________.
   neighborhood   falsehood   statehood
2. **Argument** is to **quarrel** as **settlement** is to ______________________.
   agreement   equipment   ailment
3. **Handwriting** is to **penmanship** as **studying** is to ______________________.
   partnership   friendship   scholarship
4. **Tourist** is to **traveler** as **community** is to ______________________.
   installment   neighborhood   championship
5. **Sweet** is to **sour** as **truth** is to ______________________.
   falsehood   likelihood   childhood
6. **Wood** is to **house** as **cement** is to ______________________.
   measurement   enlargement   pavement
7. **Boat** is to **seamanship** as **baseball** is to ______________________.
   kinship   sportsmanship   authorship
8. **Date** is to **appointment** as **sickness** is to ______________________.
   payment   retirement   ailment
9. **Stop** is to **go** as **boredom** is to ______________________.
   excitement   enrollment   engagement
10. **Change** is to **improvement** as **fix** is to ______________________.
    assignment   adjustment   advancement

Name ______________________________

Rule The suffixes **able** and **ible** can change a noun or a verb into an adjective.

EXAMPLES

Suffix	Meaning	Word
able, or ible	able to be	break**able**, digest**ible**
able	full of	favor**able**, charit**able**

Directions Circle the base word in each underlined word. Then use the base word and the suffix in parentheses to form the word that will complete each sentence.

1. Something that can be repaired is ______________. (able)
2. Something that can be reversed is ______________. (ible)
3. Something that you liked was ______________. (able)
4. Something that can be reproduced is ______________. (ible)
5. Something that can be insured is ______________. (able)
6. Something that can be converted is ______________. (ible)
7. Something that can be deducted is ______________. (ible)
8. Something that can be enjoyed is ______________. (able)

Directions Now use one of the words you wrote to complete each sentence.

1. My brother, Joe, bought a car with a soft, ______________ top.
2. The car needs some work, but Joe believes it is ______________.
3. When Joe drives with the top down, he wears his ______________ jacket.
4. He always has an ______________ time in his car!

Directions Read the base words in the box. Use each base word and suffix to form a new word that will complete one of the sentences. If the base word ends in **e,** drop the **e** before adding a suffix beginning with a vowel.

break (able)	flex (ible)	read (able)	enjoy (able)
like (able)	wash (able)	favor (able)	response (ible)
play (able)	depend (able)	inflate (able)	convert (ible)

1. Tammy thinks her baby-sitting job is quite ______________.

2. She works for the Manns, who find her extremely ______________.

3. Tammy works each weekend, but her hours are ______________.

4. The two children enjoy Tammy's company because she is ______________.

5. Tammy never allows them to play with anything ______________.

6. She helps them practice their printing so it will be ______________.

7. They listen to records so old that they are barely ______________.

8. Tammy takes the children outside when weather conditions are

______________.

9. When the children play in the pool, Tammy floats on an ______________ raft.

10. Tammy is teaching the children to be more ______________.

11. After meals, she asks them to soak any dishes that are ______________.

12. The Manns drive Tammy home in their ______________.

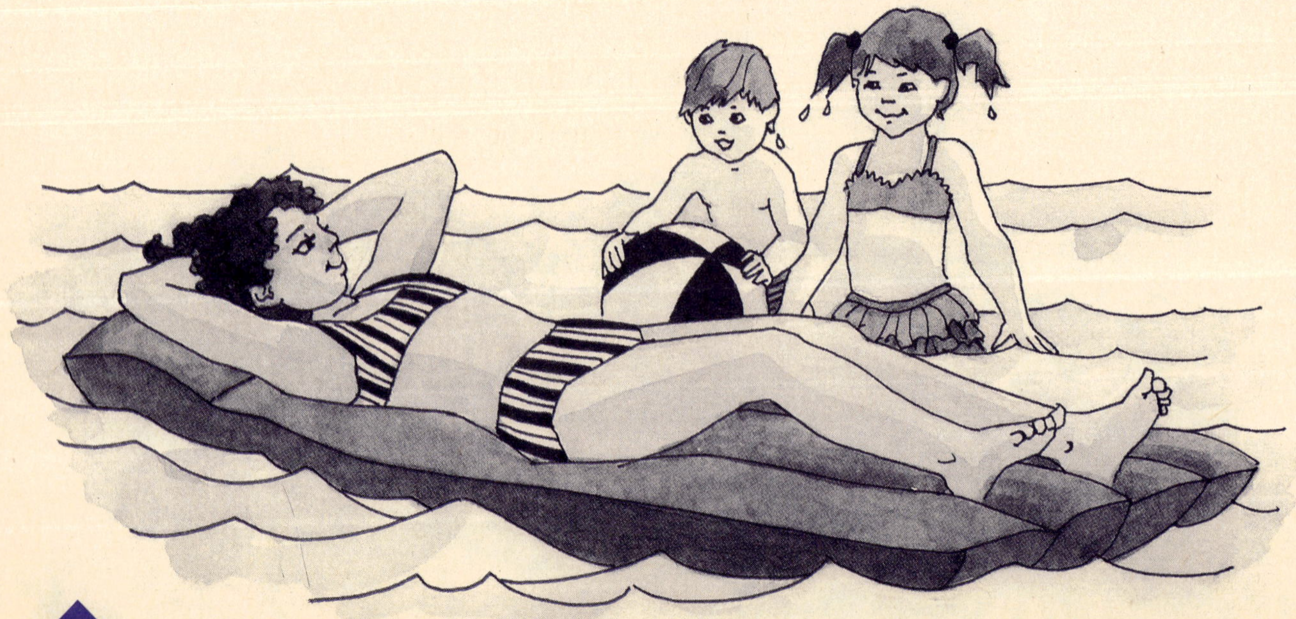

Name ____________________

Rule The suffixes **ion**, **ation**, and **ition** usually mean the *act of* or a *condition of being*. Each of these suffixes can change a verb into a noun.

EXAMPLES

Word	Meaning
connec**tion**	condition of being connected
add**ition**	act of adding
present**ation**	act of presenting

Directions Read the words in the box. Notice that there are a noun and a verb in each pair. Choose the word that best completes each definition.

tax, taxation	relate, relation	locate, location	admire, admiration
obstruct, obstruction	erupt, eruption	select, selection	reject, rejection
	compose, composition		

1. something written to be read or played on a musical instrument

   ____

2. to add an extra amount to the price of something

   ____

3. a sudden burst of lava and rock from a volcano

   ____

4. a place

   ____

5. a large barrier or thing that blocks

   ____

6. to think well of, respect

   ____

7. the choosing of something

   ____

8. to refuse or not accept

   ____

9. any family member

   ____

Directions Add a word from the box to the suffix to complete each sentence. If the base word ends in **e,** drop the **e** before adding it to the suffix.

expect	vibrate	destruct	converse	present
add	combine	locate	inform	populate

1. Our Midwestern ________________**ion** makes us a prime target for tornadoes.
2. Yesterday we waited in nervous ________________**ation** of a fierce tornado's arrival.
3. Its ________________**ation** of speed and whirling air made it a menace.
4. It had struck a nearby town, creating widespread ________________**ion.**
5. Thankfully, no one in the town's ________________**ion** was injured.
6. In the basement, we could feel the ________________**ion** of the winds.
7. We kept the radio on, listening attentively for further ________________**ation.**
8. News broadcasts featured the ________________**ition** of safety procedure stories.
9. We felt too anxious to engage in any ________________**ation.**
10. We cheered as a news ________________**ation** finally stated that the tornado had bypassed us.

Name ____________________

Rule The suffixes **ance** and **ence** usually mean the *quality or state of being.*

Examples

clear**ance** = state of being cleared

depend**ence** = quality of being dependent

These suffixes can change a verb into a noun.

Rule The suffix **ity** can mean the *quality, condition, or fact of being.*

Examples

sincer**ity** = quality of being sincere

This suffix can change an adjective into a noun.

Rule The suffix **ive** means *likely to or having to do with.*

Examples

impress**ive** = likely to impress

This suffix can change a verb into an adjective.

Directions Read each paragraph. Underline each word that has the suffix **ance, ence, ity,** or **ive.** The words you underline must contain a base word or a root and a suffix.

The number of students in attendance at the prom was higher this year than last. As the band played with magnificence, all the dancers came alive. Many creative steps were inspired by the wonderful music. What a pity that I don't have more mobility myself. But I showed what great competence I have for pouring punch!

The detective looked for clues at the scene of the crime. The thief had gained admittance through the sliding door. Then he or she had escaped over the back fence. The bees' hive in the garden had been knocked over. The tracks were suggestive of a thief heading toward the city. After checking leads in the city, the clues faded into obscurity. The detective could not deduce a motive. In reality nothing had been taken from the residence.

Directions Now write one of the words from those you underlined above on each line next to its definition.

1. great freedom of movement ____________________

2. the right to enter ____________________

3. place to live ____________________

4. full of imagination ____________________

Directions Words with the suffixes **ance, ence, ity,** or **ive** are hidden in the puzzle. The words can go across or down. Circle each word as you find it. Then write it on one of the lines.

```
P U A A C T I V I T Y C
B E A S I O O C G H R O
F X O A L L I A N C E N
J C D A Q E B Z A G A F
M E D B D R C N C H Z I
M L I K B A Y D T Y O D
A L T E R N A T I V E E
S E Y T W C U E V L G N
S N R K N E X J E T P C
I C A U T O M O T I V E
V E P R O D U C T I V E
E C M W M A T U R I T Y
```

Name ______________________________

Directions Use the words in the box to complete the letter.

allowance	neighborhood	application	education
population	advertisement	impressive	vacation
retirement	university	enjoyable	information

Dear Ray,

How do you like your new home and ______________ (1)? I found ______________ (2) in my encyclopedia that says the ______________ (3) of your new city is 150,000.

I have a story to tell you. I think you will find it ______________ (4). I saw an ______________ (5) in the newspaper for a job at the zoo. You know I've been looking for a job because I need more money than my weekly ______________ (6) pays me. So I filled out an ______________ (7) for the job. When I went in for an interview, they said they didn't pay very much. Do you know why? It's because they have an excellent ______________ (8) program with lots of benefits. Since I'm only sixteen, I'm not thinking about retirement right now; however, I may take the job anyway if they offer it to me.

I hope you will think about coming back here for your ______________ (9) after high school. We could go to the ______________ (10) together. They have very ______________ (11) courses in medicine.

See you during summer ______________ (12).

Your friend,

Dana

Directions Read each statement. Each one could be the first sentence in an article written to persuade. Choose one of the sentences and write a short paragraph made up of three or four sentences to persuade someone to do something. In your sentences, use words that have the suffixes **hood, ship, ment, ance, ence, ity, ive, able, ible, ion, ation,** or **ition.**

1. There are three good reasons why you should have a membership in the math club.
2. It would be a great idea to take Mrs. Clark's class in communication skills.
3. Our bicycle tune-up is just what you need—here's why!
4. Selling our T-shirts to your friends can be a profitable business for you.

Directions Now write the words from your sentences that contain any of the suffixes listed in the directions at the top.

Name ______________________________

Directions Read the words. Then make new words by adding the suffix above each column.

Rule When a short-vowel word ends in a single consonant, usually double the consonant before adding a suffix that begins with a vowel.

	er	ed	ing
1. trap	________	________	________
2. drum	________	________	________
3. blot	________	________	________
4. chop	________	________	________
5. bat	________	________	________
6. ship	________	________	________

Directions Read the words in the box and circle their base words. Then choose two words from the box to complete each sentence.

swimmers	batter	joggers	sitting	sunny	clapping
stopped	letting	running	getting	wettest	scanning

1. Yesterday was the ________ day of the year, but the rain finally ________.

2. Today people are ________ themselves enjoy the ________ weather.

3. At the track, ________ are ________ some exercise.

4. The lifeguard at the pool is ________ the ________.

5. At the baseball game, the ________ is ________ toward second base.

6. The people ________ in the bleachers are ________.

Directions Circle each base word that ends in a single consonant. Then form new words by putting the base words and suffixes together. Write the words on the lines.

1.	slip	______ er	______ ing	______ ed
2.	bag	______ er	______ age	______ ed
3.	glad	______ ly	______ ness	______ est
4.	scrub	______ er	______ ing	______ ed
5.	big	______ er	______ est	______ ness
6.	jog	______ er	______ ed	______ ing
7.	slim	______ ing	______ er	______ est
8.	arm	______ ful	______ ed	______ ing
9.	mad	______ en	______ er	______ ness
10.	pack	______ ed	______ ing	______ er
11.	ship	______ ers	______ ed	______ ing
12.	fit	______ er	______ ful	______ ing
13.	can	______ ed	______ ing	______ er
14.	rent	______ er	______ ed	______ ing
15.	rip	______ ed	______ ing	______ er
16.	flap	______ ing	______ ed	______ er
17.	chill	______ y	______ ing	______ ed
18.	sharp	______ er	______ en	______ ness
19.	map	______ ed	______ ing	______ s
20.	clean	______ er	______ est	______ ing
21.	drop	______ ing	______ ed	______ er
22.	wild	______ ly	______ er	______ est
23.	flat	______ er	______ est	______ en
24.	fog	______ ed	______ ing	______ y
25.	slug	______ ing	______ er	______ ed
26.	long	______ est	______ ing	______ er

Name ______________________________

Directions Form new words by adding the suffixes.

Rule When a word ends in final **e**, usually drop the **e** before adding a suffix that begins with a vowel. Do not usually drop the **e** when adding a suffix that begins with a consonant.

1. migrate + ion ____________

2. divide + er ____________

3. grave + est ____________

4. dance + ing ____________

5. polite + ness ____________

6. ripe + ness ____________

7. hesitate + ion ____________

8. secure + ly ____________

9. wrinkle + ed ____________

10. believe + able ____________

Directions Read each sentence. Circle each word that drops the final **e** to add a suffix. Then write the base word of each circled word on the lines.

1. The latest grade Gary received in math wasn't very good.

2. He decided it was desirable to work harder.

3. He hoped to do better and believed he could do it.

4. Everyone was amazed at his determination.

5. Mr. Martin, his teacher, praised him as he improved.

6. Gary derived great pleasure from his continued success.

Directions Form new words by adding suffixes. Remember, usually drop the final **e** if the suffix begins with a vowel.

1.	startle + ed	________	**2.**	have + ing	________
3.	mobile + ity	________	**4.**	elevate + or	________
5.	write + ing	________	**6.**	blue + est	________
7.	compute + er	________	**8.**	sincere + ly	________
9.	hope + ful	________	**10.**	appreciate + ed	________
11.	decide + ed	________	**12.**	describe + able	________
13.	practice + ed	________	**14.**	improve + ment	________
15.	forgive + ness	________	**16.**	guide + ance	________

Directions Complete each sentence with one of the words you wrote.

1. Sarah helped Sue learn to use her new ________.
2. Sue wanted to use it for ________ school papers.
3. She ________ Sarah's help and wanted to do something for her in return.
4. She knew Sarah played softball but was ________ trouble with her hitting.
5. If Sarah could show an ________, she might make the team.
6. Sue was the team's best hitter, so she ________ to help Sarah.
7. She was ________ that Sarah could do it.
8. The two girls ________ together every day.
9. With Sue's ________, Sarah worked hard and made the team.

Name ______________________________

Rule Many words have more than one suffix.

Additional suffixes are added according to the rules you have learned:

1) When a word ends in final **e**, usually drop the **e** before adding a suffix that begins with a vowel.

2) Do not usually drop the **e** when adding a suffix that begins with a consonant.

Directions Underline the first suffix and draw a circle around the second suffix. Remember, **s** can be a suffix.

1. hardened	**2.** foolishness	**3.** vacations	**4.** fearfulness
5. tearfully	**6.** courageously	**7.** legalized	**8.** thoughtfully
9. peacefulness	**10.** adoptions	**11.** actions	**12.** moistened

Directions Read each sentence. Fill in the circle beside the word with more than one suffix that completes the sentence. Then write the base words on the lines below.

1. When Carla ____, she found a beautiful package on the edge of her bed.
❍ stretched ❍ awakened ❍ looked

2. Carla looked at the package ____.
❍ seriously ❍ curiously ❍ expectantly

3. She opened it very ____.
❍ cautiously ❍ carefully ❍ easily

4. Carla didn't want to ____ break anything.
❍ suddenly ❍ accidentally ❍ horribly

5. Seeing the gift, she was ____.
❍ happy ❍ heartened ❍ excited

6. ____, it was exactly what she wanted.
❍ Amazingly ❍ Surely ❍ Certainly

7. Grandma always ____ knew what she wanted.
❍ somehow ❍ mysteriously ❍ exactly

8. Carla thanked Grandma for her ____.
❍ thoughtfulness ❍ generosity ❍ kindness

1. ____________ **2.** ____________ **3.** ____________ **4.** ____________

5. ____________ **6.** ____________ **7.** ____________ **8.** ____________

Directions Combine each base word with the two suffixes.

thought + ful + ness	______________	sharp + en + ed	______________
awake + en + ed	______________	fear + ful + ness	______________
truth + ful + ness	______________	celebrate + ion + s	______________
amaze + ing + ly	______________	power + less + ness	______________
thank + ful + ness	______________	cheer + ful + ly	______________
wide + en + ing	______________	favor + able + ly	______________
fright + en + ing	______________	hope + ful + ly	______________

Directions Use the words you wrote to complete the following sentences.

1. A person who never lies or cheats has the virtue of ______________.
2. A synonym for happily is ______________.
3. An antonym of powerfulness is ______________.
4. The alarm clock ______________ everyone at 6 o'clock this morning.
5. A synonym for scary is ______________.
6. A pencil with a broken point needs to be ______________.
7. The traffic had to follow a detour because the road crews were ______________ the street.
8. There were many ______________ in our town when the high school football team won the championship.
9. Someone who is afraid may be in a state of ______________.
10. To be in agreement with something means to react ______________ to it.

Name ______________________________

Directions Study the examples. Then complete the rules.

Forming Plurals		Adding Other Suffixes	
study—studies	valley—valleys	funny—funnier	occupy—occupying
story—stories	bay—bays	heavy—heaviest	obey—obeyed

1. If a word ends in **y** preceded by a consonant, make it plural by changing the **y** to ______ and adding the letters ______.
2. If a word ends in **y** preceded by a vowel, make it plural by adding ______.
3. If a word ends in **y** preceded by a consonant, change the letter ______ to ______ before adding any suffix except **ing.**
4. If a word ends in **y** preceded by a ______________, just add the suffix.

Directions Combine each base word and suffix. Then write the new word to complete each sentence.

1. Mike and Jeff went to the carnival and (stay + ed) ________________ until closing time.
2. Mike went on more rides than Jeff, so he felt (dizzy + er) ________________.
3. They both agreed that a new ride, The Tornado, was the (scary + est) ________________.
4. They (try + ed) ________________ their luck at the games and won some prizes.
5. Mike and Jeff both had a very (enjoy + able) ________________ time.
6. There were so many (activity + s) ________________, they wished they could stay longer.
7. They made plans to return on one of the following (day + s) ________________.

Directions Make new words by adding the suffixes.

spy + es	______________	occupy + es	______________
pry + ed	______________	canary + es	______________
lazy + er	______________	healthy + est	______________
sky + es	______________	turkey + s	______________
bossy + er	______________	study + ed	______________
sentry + es	______________	dirty + er	______________

Directions Use the words you wrote to complete the crossword puzzle.

Across

2. tried to learn
4. lives in
6. guards
9. more covered with grime
10. large birds that are eaten by many people on Thanksgiving Day

Down

1. having the best health of all
2. people who keep secret watch on the actions of others
3. more fond of telling others what to do and how to do it
5. small yellow birds that sing sweetly
7. the heavens
8. raised, moved, or forced with a lever

Name ____

Directions Study the examples. Then complete the rules.

heavy + ly = heavily	wobble + ly = wobbly
cheery + ly = cheerily	feeble + ly = feebly

1. When a word ends in **y** preceded by a consonant, follow this rule to add the suffix **ly:**

   Change the letter _____ to _____ before adding **ly.**

2. When a word ends in **le,** follow this rule to add the suffix **ly:**

   Drop the letters _____ and add **ly.**

Directions Add the suffix **ly** to each word. Then complete the sentences using words you formed.

1. easy __________	**2.** possible __________	**3.** lucky __________
4. simple __________	**5.** probable __________	**6.** noble __________
7. bubble __________	**8.** hearty __________	**9.** hasty __________
10. sleepy __________	**11.** nimble __________	**12.** wiggle __________

1. Jenny wasn't fully awake yet, so she ______________ got out of bed.
2. She realized she had overslept and ______________ tried to get ready.
3. She couldn't ______________ be late for school today.
4. The spelling bee was first thing, and she ______________ had to be there.
5. Jenny knew she was a good speller and would ______________ win.
6. ______________ the school bus was a little late, so she caught it in time.
7. Jenny is such a good speller that she ______________ won the spelling bee.

Directions Choose a word from the box that fits each clue and write it on the line. Then circle each word you wrote in the puzzle below. Some of the words in the puzzle go across, and others go down.

heavily	wobbly	simply	greedily	ably	busily
prickly	saucily	pebbly	easily	sleepily	happily
nimbly	weepily	sparkly	sloppily	crackly	nobly
angrily	drizzly	dizzily	feebly	lazily	wiggly

1. ______________ how some people act when they are furious
2. ______________ weather that is damp and misty
3. ______________ the way an ocean beach filled with small stones looks
4. ______________ how a person who never wants to work acts
5. ______________ very actively
6. ______________ like a chair that would move from side to side if you sat on it
7. ______________ how fireworks look
8. ______________ how fire sounds
9. ______________ how a selfish person acts

```
A N B R G W O B B L Y D E R
S A N G R I L Y D E P R I V
P B A B E C P D F W A I M G
A U A I E I E K A L R Z M Z
R S G S D R B L S D I Z G I
K I U V I P B W B L M L A L
L L G R L B L A Z I L Y T U
Y Y H M Y Z Y C R A C K L Y
```

Name ____

Directions Complete the story by adding suffixes to form new words.

Whistler's mother, Anna McNeill Whistler, may be one of the most ____________ (recognize + able) ________ (lady + es) in history because of the portrait her son ________ (able + ly) painted. James Whistler often ____________ (disagree + ed) with his ____________ (extreme + ly) strict mother. Yet he greatly ________ (admire + ed) her sympathetic ____________ (quality + es) and praised her ______________ (kindhearted + ness) to others. For example, Anna Whistler ________ (devote + ed) herself to ________ (nurse + ing) twenty bedridden people before they died. James Whistler's feelings were also ________ (stir + ed) by his mother's face.

In her face, he saw "grace ________ (wed + ed) to dignity, strength ____________ (enhance + ing) sweetness."

Whistler ________ (decide + ed) to paint his mother's portrait when she was sixty-five. She ________ (model + ed) in a black dress and ______________ (white-lace + ed) bonnet. She was ____________ (require + ed) to be ____________ (motion + less) for long hours while her son ________ (busy + ly) painted. Though the portrait is now famous, there were no ________ (buy + ers) for it, at first. ________ (Final + ly), Whistler sold it to a museum for $625. Today it is a ____________ (price + less) work of art.

Directions Write **yes** or **no** to answer each question.

1. ______ Have many people seen the portrait of Whistler's mother?
2. ______ Did James Whistler almost always agree with his mother?
3. ______ Did James think his mother was a kind woman?
4. ______ Did James see prettiness and girlishness in his mother's face?
5. ______ Did the bonnet in the portrait have white lace?
6. ______ Did Anna Whistler need to sit very still while modeling?

Directions Read the article and then answer the questions.

Definition An **outline** can help you summarize an article for study. A **topic outline** uses nouns and short phrases to state the main ideas.

James Whistler is considered one of the best American artists of the 1800s. He was born in 1834 in Massachusetts. When he was nine, he moved with his family to Russia. Later his family moved back to the United States, and Whistler studied art in the East. At the age of twenty-two, he moved to France and seriously devoted himself to art. London, England, became his permanent home after 1859.

Whistler created many paintings, etchings, and lithographs. His most famous painting is commonly known as *Whistler's Mother.* Other important works are *The White Girl, Self-Portrait,* and *The Ocean*.

1. In what places did Whistler make his **residence?**

______________ ______________

______________ ______________ ______________

2. What were some of Whistler's most **famous paintings?**

______________ ______________

______________ ______________

Directions Complete the outline. Use the words in boldface print above to help you write the headings. Then use the answers to the questions to help write the topics, or main facts.

James Whistler

I. Residences

A. ______________

B. ______________

C. ______________

D. ______________

E. ______________

II. ______________

A. ______________

B. ______________

C. ______________

D. ______________

Name ____________________

Rules If a word ends in **f** or **fe**, usually change the **f** or **fe** to **v** and add **es** to make the word plural. Exceptions to this rule are **chief**, **belief**, **reef**, and **roof**. A word that ends in **ff** is made plural by adding **s**.

EXAMPLES

Singular	Plural
wolf	wolves
knife	knives
cliff	cliffs
chief	chiefs

Directions Write the plural form of each word.

puff ______	elf ______	cuff ______
hoof ______	thief ______	knife ______
muff ______	wolf ______	calf ______
scarf ______	roof ______	reef ______
sniff ______	cliff ______	staff ______
chief ______	sheaf ______	life ______

Directions For each clue or definition below, write the correct plural word.

1. ______ horses' feet
2. ______ baby cattle
3. ______ cutting instruments
4. ______ heads of tribes
5. ______ what your nose does
6. ______ tops of houses
7. ______ wild animals, similar to dogs
8. ______ outlaws who steal
9. ______ bands around the wrists
10. ______ tiny imaginary folk
11. ______ cloths worn on the head or neck
12. ______ ridges of rocks in an ocean or lake, often made of coral
13. ______ steep sides of rocks
14. ______ shorts bursts of smoke or steam
15. ______ sticks or poles used for support when walking

Directions Write the plural word that describes each picture.

1.

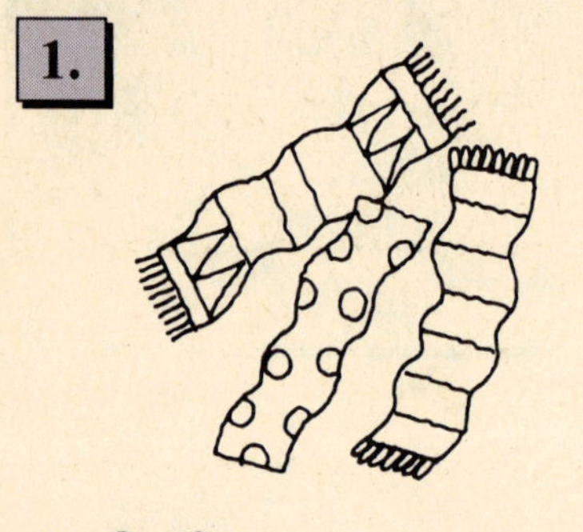

s c __________

2.

c __________

3.

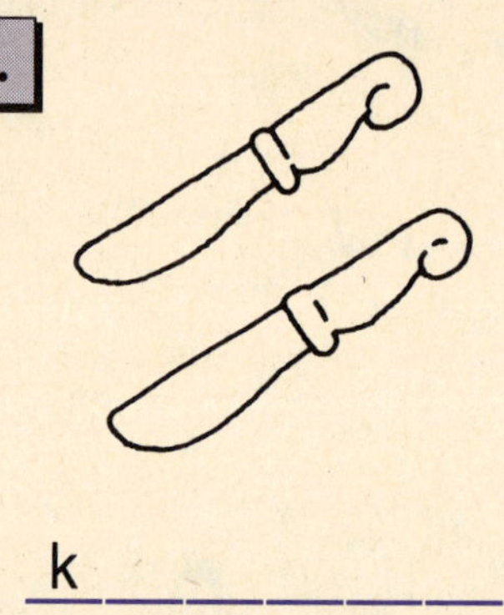

k __________

4.

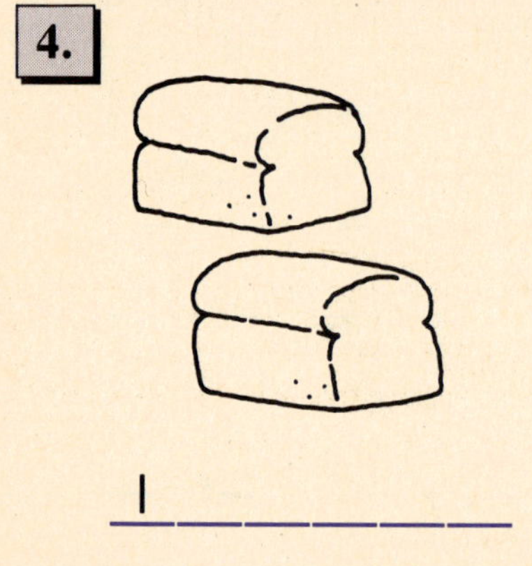

l __________

5.

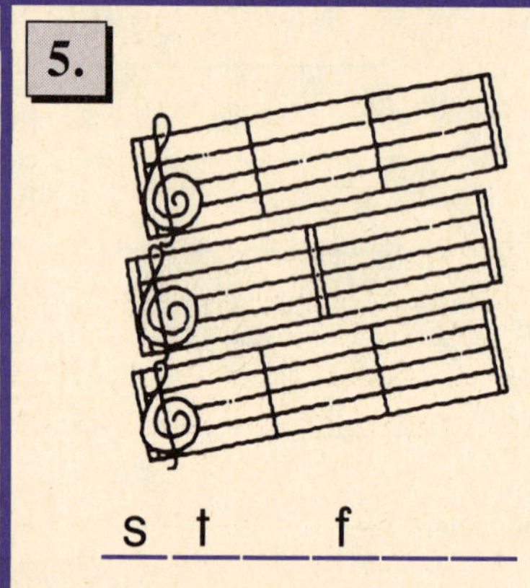

s t _ f __________

6.

c __________

7.

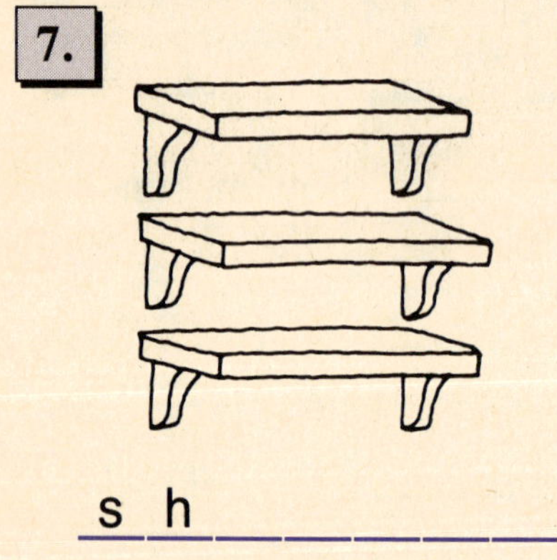

s h __________

8.

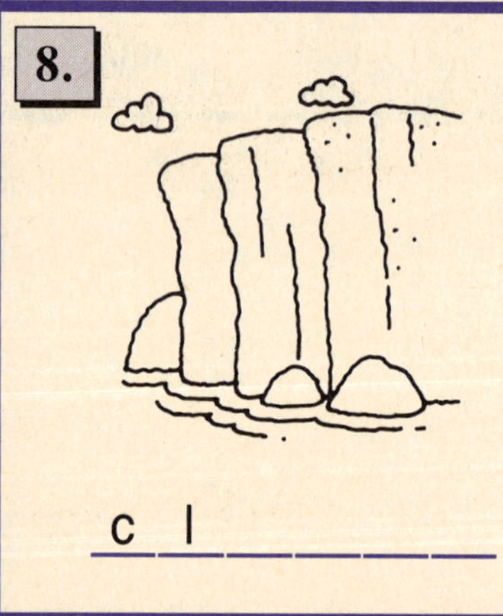

c l __________

9.

w __________

10.

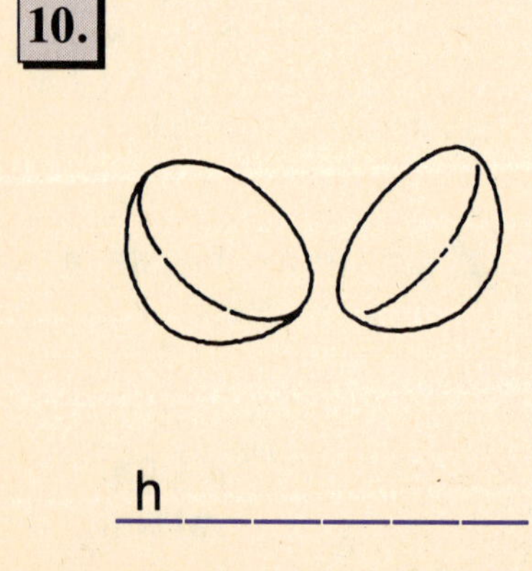

h __________

11.

l __________

12.

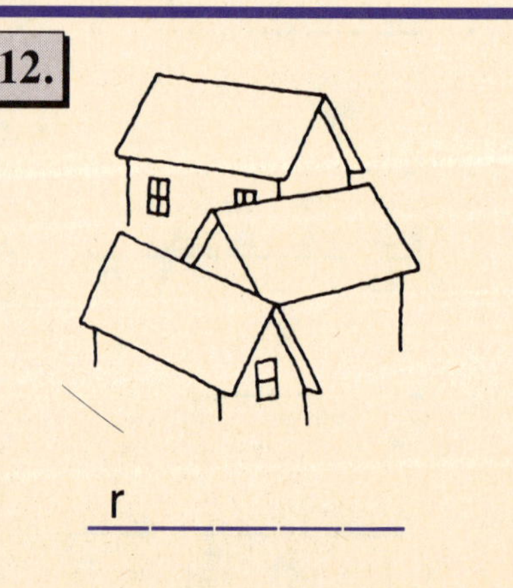

r __________

Name ______________________________

Rule If a word ends in **o**, an s is usually added to make the word plural. Some exceptions are made plural by adding **es**.

EXAMPLES

potato—potatoes
buffalo—buffaloes
torpedo—torpedoes
echo—echoes
veto—vetoes
tornado—tornadoes

Directions Write **s** or **es** to show the plural of each word.

1. stereo ____	**2.** hero ____	**3.** photo ____	**4.** rodeo ____
5. avocado ____	**6.** piccolo ____	**7.** piano ____	**8.** tuxedo ____
9. solo ____	**10.** tempo ____	**11.** poncho ____	**12.** tomato ____
13. domino ____	**14.** burro ____	**15.** radio ____	**16.** kangaroo ____

Directions Write a plural word from above to complete each sentence.

1. At the outdoor cafe, Maria ordered chicken salad with green ______________.
2. Tina ordered tuna salad with juicy red ______________.
3. It was chilly out, so they were glad they had worn their ______________.
4. Maria brought her camera and hoped to get some ______________ of the concert.
5. They had listened to the musicians on their ______________ but had never seen them.
6. They arrived just as two men in black ______________ came onstage.
7. The men sat at ______________ and played several duets.
8. Then they took turns playing ______________.
9. Later they were joined by a quartet of flutes and ______________.
10. Tina enjoyed the ballads, but Maria liked the songs with livelier ______________.

Directions The plural forms of the words in the box will help you answer the questions. Use the plural words to complete the crossword puzzle.

photo	soprano
rodeo	solo
piano	tornado
potato	tomato
avocado	sombrero
kangaroo	torpedo

Across

1. What are red and juicy and used in making spaghetti sauce?
3. What are hopping animals found in Australia?
7. What can a photographer take?
9. What does Kansas have more of than any other state?
10. What are pieces of music for one voice or one instrument called?
11. In what kinds of contests do contestants ride horses bareback for 10 seconds?

Down

2. What are cigar-shaped missiles used under water called?
4. What do you call broad-brimmed hats that tie under the chin?
5. What are pear-shaped fruits with large pits in the middle?
6. Who are people with the highest singing voices?
7. Which vegetables taste good baked, mashed, French fried or scalloped?
8. For which instruments did Mozart and Chopin write music?

1 2 3 4 5 6 7 8 9 10 11

Name ____________________

Directions The words in the box are the same in their singular and plural forms. Choose one of the words to complete each pair of sentences.

Rule Some words do not change at all in their plural form.

sauerkraut	aircraft	spinach	spaghetti	oatmeal
salmon	chili	broccoli	trout	zucchini
scissors	series	moose	shrimp	wheat

1. A small, two engine ____________ just landed.

Three jet ____________ took off within the last ten minutes.

2. The ____________ had large antlers.

The herd of ____________ was headed toward the lake.

3. She picked a ____________ from the garden.

The recipe called for three ____________.

Rule Some words change completely in their plural form. Other plural forms may not be familiar and do not follow any of the other rules.

Examples

tooth—teeth
phylum—phyla
curriculum—curricula
octopus—octopi

Directions Complete each phrase by writing the plural of the word in parentheses. You may use your dictionary.

1. six wild ____________ (goose)

2. three lovely ____________ (woman)

3. four watery ____________ (oasis)

4. five generous ____________ (alumnus)

5. six tiny ____________ (mouse)

6. two dangerous ____________ (bacterium)

7. two tired ____________ (foot)

8. six unusual ____________ (fungus)

9. five handsome ____________ (man)

10. eight noisy ____________ (child)

Directions Complete the sentences with the plural forms of the words in parentheses.

1. The Smiths and the Carters were going to the college's ________________ (alumnus) picnic.

2. That morning, the Carters' daughter lost two loose ________________ (tooth).

3. Mrs. Smith saw two ________________ (mouse) in her basement while getting the picnic basket.

4. Despite these ________________ (crisis), both families were ready to leave on schedule.

5. The picnic ground was near the woods, and they saw some ________________ (deer).

6. There was a lake nearby with more ________________ (goose) than they had ever seen.

7. The ________________ (woman) had made sandwiches and brought ________________ (popcorn) for snacks.

8. Their husbands had made a salad of ________________ (spinach), ________________ (zucchini), and tomatoes.

9. After lunch, the ________________ (man) decided to take advantage of the fishing.

10. They had fished for ________________ (salmon) but had never fished for ________________ (trout) before.

11. The ________________ (child) hiked through the woods until their ________________ (foot) hurt.

12. They were sure they had spotted two ________________ (moose) with big antlers.

13. They were told that they probably had seen ________________ (elk).

14. The highlight was scenic flights over the lake in two ________________ (aircraft).

Name ______________________________

Directions Write a word from the box to complete each sentence. Then list each word under the correct heading.

apologized	misunderstanding	disagreements	realized	appreciated
endangered	unfortunately	sympathetic	unpleasant	understood

1. Sometimes friends have serious ______________________.
2. ______________________, it happened to John and Carl.
3. For two days, there were ______________________ feelings between them.
4. Then John ______________________ that he had treated Carl unfairly.
5. He knew he had ______________________ their friendship.
6. He wanted to clear up the ______________________.
7. He ______________________ to Carl for misjudging him.
8. Carl ______________________ how John could have made the mistake.
9. John ______________________ Carl's understanding.
10. It was good to have a friend who was so ______________________.

Three syllables

____

____

____

____

Four syllables

____

____

____

Five syllables

____

____

____

Rule Divide a compound word between the words that make the compound word.

Examples

tea/pot like/wise never/the/less

Rule When a word ends in **le** preceded by a consonant, divide the word before that consonant.

Examples

a/ble bea/gle tin/gle

Directions Find the word in each pair that ends in **le** or is a compound word, and divide it into syllables, using vertical lines. Write **S** on the line if the words are synonyms, or mean the same. Write **A** if they are antonyms, or have opposite meanings.

1. giggle/laugh ___	**2.** tumble/fall ___	**3.** park/playground ___
4. snapshot/photo ___	**5.** handbag/purse ___	**6.** stifle/stop ___
7. shake/tremble ___	**8.** worthwhile/useless ___	**9.** fable/story ___
10. sweetheart/enemy ___	**11.** lowly/noble ___	**12.** glitter/sparkle ___
13. strong/feeble ___	**14.** chew/nibble ___	**15.** uncle/aunt ___
16. unfit/able ___	**17.** hardship/luxury ___	**18.** battle/fight ___
19. arouse/kindle ___	**20.** gigantic/little ___	**21.** forever/enduring ___
22. breakdown/collapse ___	**23.** grasslands/plains ___	**24.** proud/humble ___
25. pebble/stone ___	**26.** foolproof/complex ___	**27.** nimble/spry ___
28. agree/quibble ___	**29.** into/out ___	**30.** stable/disrupted ___
31. cottontail/rabbit ___	**32.** gentle/harsh ___	**33.** contend/wrestle ___

Name ______________________________

Directions Study the rules. Then read each sentence and divide the two words in boldface print into syllables, using vertical lines.

Rule When two or more consonants come between two vowels, the word is usually divided between the first two consonants.

EXAMPLES

bet/ter	suf/fer
pic/ture	har/ness

Rule When a single consonant comes between two vowels, the word is usually divided after the consonant if the first vowel is short.

EXAMPLES

clev/er	lem/on
rob/in	trav/el

Rule When a single consonant comes between two vowels, the word is usually divided before the consonant if the first vowel is long.

EXAMPLES

ma/jor	ra/zor
pri/vate	le/gal

1. It was a **sunny** day for a **picnic.** ____________ ____________
2. A group of friends went to the park that was **beyond** the **forest.** ____________ ____________
3. Jack had **never** been there **before.** ____________ ____________
4. Jane said to **follow** her through the **tunnel.** ____________ ____________
5. Maria and Adam brought their **tennis racquets.** ____________ ____________
6. Jane spread out the **yellow blanket.** ____________ ____________
7. Adam was **hungry** and opened the **basket.** ____________ ____________
8. He took out the **napkins** and **paper** plates. ____________ ____________
9. They had cheese sandwiches with **lettuce** and **olives.** ____________ ____________
10. For dessert they ate some **melon** that had a very sweet **flavor.** ____________ ____________

Rule When a compound word has more than two syllables, first divide between the words that make up the compound word. Then divide the smaller words into syllables.

EXAMPLES

flow/er/pot	ev/er/y/bod/y
win/dow/pane	fin/ger/print

Rule When a word has more than two syllables, figure out how many syllables it has. Then divide it into syllables according to the rules you have learned.

EXAMPLES

an/gri/ly	av/o/ca/dos
pro/nun/ci/a/tion	sub/ur/ban

Directions Write the number of syllables you hear in the word. Then use vertical lines to divide the word into syllables.

expertly	___	______________	expression	___	______________
disbelief	___	______________	inefficient	___	______________
determination	___	______________	kangaroos	___	______________
strawberries	___	______________	shopkeeper	___	______________
inseparable	___	______________	quickened	___	______________
illegal	___	______________	drizzled	___	______________
distribution	___	______________	corporation	___	______________
windowpane	___	______________	scorekeeper	___	______________
igloos	___	______________	shredding	___	______________
operations	___	______________	irreversible	___	______________
football	___	______________	decided	___	______________
gratefully	___	______________	abilities	___	______________
battery	___	______________	geographical	___	______________
proceeded	___	______________	congratulations	___	______________
improper	___	______________	idea	___	______________
showboat	___	______________	puppeteer	___	______________
repetition	___	______________	oneself	___	______________

Name ______________________________

Directions Read the article. Complete each unfinished sentence by writing the plural form of each word on the line above it.

Since the early ____________ (day) of the colonies, ____________ (man), ____________ (woman), and ____________ (child) have enjoyed local fairs. City and county fairs are a high point in people's ____________ (life) because they offer fun and entertainment for everyone. Many people take part in ____________ (rodeo) and weightlifting. There are ____________ (pony) for the children to ride. Men and women enjoy demonstrations of new ways of cooking vegetables such as ____________ (spinach), ____________ (broccoli), ____________ (zucchini), and ____________ (potato).

The booths were the highlight of one county fair. Some of the booths were for fun and games, while others were for information. For example, one booth offered a free pamphlet about the effects of food on skin, hair, and ____________ (tooth). Another booth featured a display called "Hometown ____________ (Hero)." "Some Strange ____________ (Belief) and Customs of Our Ancestors" was another popular attraction. By looking at this display, people learned that ____________ (tomato) were once thought to be poisonous. They were called "peaches of ____________ (wolf)."

Directions Read the article. Then answer the questions.

Definition Remember, an **outline** helps you summarize the important ideas in a story or article. A **topic outline** is written with words or short phrases.

Potatoes are an ancient food. Indians in South America began growing them centuries before Europeans discovered the continent. These delicious vegetables provide us with vitamin C, iron, and protein. Many people think they are fattening, but potatoes are actually low in calories. It's what you put on them—butter or sour cream—that adds the calories!

Tomatoes also originated in South America. They are an excellent source of vitamins A and C. Tomatoes are used for countless dishes. You will find them in salads, pizza and spaghetti sauces, stews, and soups.

1. What vegetable is the first paragraph about? ______
2. Where were they grown long ago? ______
3. What nutrients do they provide? ______
4. What food is the second paragraph about? ______
5. Where did they originate? ______
6. What nutrients do they provide? ______

Directions Now use your answers to complete the outline below.

Two Terrific Vegetables

First Heading **I.** ______

A. ______

B. ______

Second Heading **II.** ______

A. ______

B. ______

Name ______________________________

Directions Read the words in each group and write them in alphabetical order.

Hint In a dictionary, the entry words are arranged in alphabetical order. When words begin with the same letter or letters, look at the next letter to decide the alphabetical order.

1. tiger table today that teach

______
______
______
______
______

2. circle cabin claim chalk ceiling

______
______
______
______
______

3. indeed illusion imagine imitate inflate

______
______
______
______
______

4. habit hadn't hammer hall hair

______
______
______
______
______

5. paddle panel painter palace pants

______
______
______
______
______

6. rear realize realist ready realm

______
______
______
______
______

Directions Number the words in each group to show the correct alphabetical order.

1.
- bungalow ___
- bundle ___
- bunt ___
- bunk ___
- bunch ___

2.
- locker ___
- locality ___
- locket ___
- locomotive ___
- locate ___

Directions Read the guide words and entry words in each column. Circle any entry words that would not be on the same page as those guide words. Then number the rest of the words in the column in alphabetical order.

Hint In the dictionary, the guide words at the top of the page show the first and last entries on the page. All the other entries on that page are in alphabetical order between those words.

ascend/auditorium		macaroni/make		swallow/swung	
______	attack	______	manager	______	swoop
______	asleep	______	machinery	______	switch
______	athlete	______	made	______	symphony
______	astonish	______	majestic	______	swam
______	artist	______	magnify	______	survey

Directions Find four words in the box that would be on the dictionary page with each pair of guide words. Write those words in alphabetical order below the guide words.

coal	level	limp	coast	coin	dark	dance
decide	date	clump	cocoa	dahlia	lift	liberty

club/coil	daily/deep	lesson/listen
______	______	______
______	______	______
______	______	______
______	______	______

Name ____________________

Directions Study the pronunciation key. Then look at the words in the box and read and say each symbol below the box. Write the word from the box that has the sound that symbol stands for. The key words in the pronunciation key will help you.

Hint The dictionary respelling beside each entry word helps you pronounce that word. The dictionary's pronunciation key shows the symbols used in the respelling.

Full Pronunciation Key

VOWEL SOUNDS

SYMBOL	KEY WORDS	SYMBOL	KEY WORDS
a	ask, fat	u	up, cut
ā	ape, date	ʉr	fur, fern
ä	car, lot		
		ə	**a** in ago
e	elf, ten		**e** in agent
er	berry, care		**e** in father
ē	even, meet		**i** in unity
			o in collect
i	is, hit		**u** in focus
ir	mirror, here		
ī	ice, fire		
ō	open, go		
ô	law, horn		
ơi	oil, point		
ơo	look, pull		
ōō	ooze, tool		
yơo	unite, cure		
yōō	cute, few		
ơu	out, crowd		

CONSONANT SOUNDS

SYMBOL	KEY WORDS	SYMBOL	KEY WORDS
b	bed, dub	ch	chin, arch
d	did, had	ŋ	ring, singer
f	fall, off	sh	she, dash
g	get, dog	th	thin, truth
h	he, ahead	*th*	then, father
j	joy, jump	zh	**s** in pleasure
k	kill, bake		
l	let, ball	'	as in (ā'b'l)
m	met, trim		
n	not, ton		
p	put, tap		
r	red, dear		
s	sell, pass		
t	top, hat		
v	vat, have		
w	will, always		
y	yet, yard		
z	zebra, haze		

rarely	spoil	sting	school	those	stern
thrift	should	treasure	pail	gallop	chart

1. g ____________________ **2.** ōō ____________________

3. ā ____________________ **4.** th ____________________

5. zh ____________________ **6.** er ____________________

7. ơi ____________________ **8.** sh ____________________

9. ŋ ____________________ **10.** *th* ____________________

11. ä ____________________ **12.** ʉr ____________________

Rule Many dictionaries use the schwa symbol (ə) for the vowel sound often heard in unaccented syllables. The pronunciation key shows the different letters that can stand for this sound.

When words have two or more syllables, some syllables are stressed, or accented, more than others. A heavy accent mark (′) in the dictionary respelling shows which syllable receives the primary, or heavier, accent. A lighter accent mark (′) shows a secondary, or lesser, accent.

Directions Use the pronunciation key and accent marks to help you say each respelling. Then read the word that goes with the respelling. Circle the letter or letters in each word that stand for the schwa sound.

1.	ə plôd′	a p p l a u d	**6.**	kən sʉrn′	c o n c e r n
2.	nes′ ə ser′ ē	n e c e s s a r y	**7.**	in sī′ klə pē′ dē ə	e n c y c l o p e d i a
3.	sul′ fər	s u l f u r	**8.**	sim plis′ ə tē	s i m p l i c i t y
4.	mōt′ ər bōt	m o t o r b o a t	**9.**	ed′ ə tər	e d i t o r
5.	i maj′ ə ner′ ē	i m a g i n a r y	**10.**	jen′ ər ə lē	g e n e r a l l y

Directions Use the pronunciation key and accent marks to help you say each respelling below. In front of the respelling, write the letter of the word that is the entry for that respelling.

____ **1.** ek′ sər sīz′
____ **2.** ə fish′ ē āt
____ **3.** kʉr′ ən sē
____ **4.** mis′ un dər stand′
____ **5.** prē′ zen tā′ shən
____ **6.** meg′ ə fōn
____ **7.** ə fek′ tiv
____ **8.** plen′ ti fəl
____ **9.** ker′ ə sēn′

a. misunderstand
b. effective
c. officiate
d. megaphone
e. exercise
f. presentation
g. currency
h. plentiful
i. kerosene

Name ____________________

Hint Many dictionaries have a short pronunciation key on every page or every other page.

a	fat	e	even	oi	oil	ch	chin	ə = a *in* ago
ā	ape	i	hit	oo	look	sh	she	e *in* agent
ä	car, lot	ir	here	o͞o	tool	th	thin	i *in* unity
e	ten	ī	bite, fire	ou	out	*th*	then	o *in* collect
er	care	ō	go	u	up	zh	leisure	u *in* focus
		ô	law, horn	ʉr	fur	ŋ	ring	

Directions Read each sentence. Use the pronunciation key and accent marks to pronounce the dictionary respelling in the sentence. Then fill in the circle beside the word that is the entry word for that respelling.

1. Scientists believe that the earliest (in hab′i tənts) of China lived in caves.
❍ inhibitions ❍ inhabitants ❍ inheritance

2. Later, scientists think, these people began to farm and keep (də mes′ tik) animals.
❍ domestic ❍ domesticated ❍ domicile

3. Several ancient settlements have been (dis kuv′ ərd) in China.
❍ disclosed ❍ discovered ❍ discouraged

4. Scientists have (ig zam′ ənd) the ruins of these settlements.
❍ examined ❍ examination ❍ excavated

5. Some of the oldest of these settlements are located in the rich (val′ ē) of the Hwang Ho River.
❍ valid ❍ valley ❍ value

6. These settlements, say the scientists, were (kən strukt′ id) as long ago as 2000 B.C.
❍ erected ❍ construction ❍ constructed

7. The people of these settlements developed a form of strong (guv′ ərn mənt).
❍ governor ❍ government ❍ governing

8. They also were able to make (bränz) tools.
❍ bronze ❍ bronzed ❍ brass

9. In time, the settlements were united into city-states and (em′pīrz).
❍ umpires ❍ employs ❍ empires

10. These were ruled for hundreds of years at a time by the family groups called (dī′ nəs tēz).
❍ dynasties ❍ dialogues ❍ diamonds

Directions Read each word in boldface print. Beside it, write the entry word you would look for in the dictionary.

Hint Entry words do not usually have the suffixes and spelling changes that words can have when we use them in sentences. Most spelling changes appear at the beginning or at the end of the entry.

1. striding ____________
2. compliments ____________
3. enraged ____________
4. guiltily ____________
5. resistance ____________
6. geese ____________
7. connected ____________
8. driving ____________
9. sang ____________
10. jetties ____________

Directions Read the paragraphs. Notice the numbered words in boldface print. Write each numbered word as you would find it as a dictionary entry word.

Mongolia is **located** (1) east of the Chinese province of Sinkiang. Within Mongolia is the Gobi Desert, one of the **largest** (2) desert areas in the world. **Steppes,** (3) where most of the population live, surround the Gobi. For **centuries,** (4) the people of Mongolia have **kept** (5) herds of livestock on these steppes.

Present-day Mongolians live mostly by tending the herds. Their **ancestors,** (6) Mongols, were among the **world's** (7) most **feared** (8) warriors. In the 1100s and 1200s, their leader, Genghis Khan, and his **successors** (9) **led** (10) these warriors on military **conquests** (11) that reached from Europe to Southeast Asia to the Middle East. In fact, the famous Great Wall of China was **built** (12) in an unsuccessful attempt to keep the Mongol warriors out of China.

1. ____________
2. ____________
3. ____________
4. ____________
5. ____________
6. ____________
7. ____________
8. ____________
9. ____________
10. ____________
11. ____________
12. ____________

Name ____

Directions Read the dictionary entries. Then use the words to complete the paragraphs. Write the correct word and its definition number on the line to complete each unfinished sentence.

Rule In the dictionary when there is more than one meaning for an entry word, numbers separate the different definitions. The meaning listed first is usually the most commonly used.

accident (ak′ sə dənt) **n.** **1.** a happening that is not expected or planned. **2.** fortune; chance.

building (bil′ ding) **n.** **1.** anything that is built with walls and a roof; a structure, as a house, factory, or school. **2.** the act or work of one who builds.

capital (kap′ ə t′l) **n.** **1.** a city or town where the government of a state or nation is located. **2.** money or property, especially when used in business to make more money.

center (sen′ tər) **n.** **1.** a point inside a circle or sphere that is the same distance from all points on the circumference or surface. **2.** the middle point or part; place at the middle. **3.** a main point or place, where there is much activity or attention.

construction (kən struk′ shən) **n.** **1.** the act of constructing or building. **2.** the way in which something is constructed or put together.

goods (goodz) **n. pl.** **1.** things made to be sold; wares. **2.** personal property that can be moved.

port (pôrt) **n.** **1.** another word for harbor. **2.** a city with a harbor where ships can load and unload.

Lima is Peru's largest city. It has almost one-fourth of the country's population. It also is Peru's economic and administrative ____________________. Most of the manufactured ____________________ produced in Peru are made in Lima and other cities along the coast. The nearby ____________________ of Callao contributes with its fisheries and petroleum refineries.

Unlike many other cities, Lima did not simply happen by ____________________. It was founded in 1535 by Francisco Pizarro. After conquering the Inca inhabitants of Peru, Pizarro looked for a place that would be in the ____________________ of the lands he had captured for the Spanish empire. He decided against using the Inca royal city of Cusco. Instead he ordered the ____________________ of a new city nearer to the sea and more convenient for land transportation.

Pizarro's city became known as the City of Kings. It was famous for its carefully planned ____________________. Its orderly system of streets and the careful arrangement of its official ____________________ made it a showplace among the cities of Spain's American empire. Today the City of Kings is called Lima.

Directions Read these entries. Decide which word to use to complete each sentence below. Write the word and its number on the line in the sentence.

Rule An entry word may have a raised number to the right. This tells you that there is another word spelled the same way that has a different meaning or origin.

close[1] (klōs) **adj.** stuffy and full of stale air.
close[2] (klōz) **v.** to make no longer open; shut.
desert[1] (di zʉrt′) **v.** to go away from someone or something that one ought not to leave.
desert[2] (dez′ ərt) **n.** a dry sandy region with little or no plant life.
desert[3] (di zʉrt′) **n.** what a person deserves, either as reward or punishment.

elder[1] (el′dər) **adj.** older.
elder[2] (el′ dər) **n.** a shrub or tree with small, white flowers and red or purple berries.
prune[1] (pro͞on) **n.** a plum dried for eating.
prune[2] (pro͞on) **v.** to cut off or trim branches, twigs, etc., from.

1. My ____________ sister Kara visited me last Saturday.
2. When she arrived, I was ____________ the bushes.
3. "I'm spring cleaning; don't ____________ me," I teased.
4. "I'll trim this overgrown ____________," Kara replied.
5. When we cleaned the attic, it felt very ____________.
6. I tried the ____________ window, but it was jammed.
7. After our chores, Kara and I snacked on ____________.

Name ______________________________

Directions Practice your dictionary skills. Read these entries and do what each sentence tells you to do.

advanced [əd vanst′] **adj.** **1.** in advance; in front. **2.** ahead of the times or of other people.

architecture [är′ kə tek′ chər] **n.** **1.** the science or work of planning and putting up buildings. **2.** a style or special way of building.

arrive [ə rīv′] **v.** to come to a place after a journey.

calendar [kal′ ən dər] **n.** **1.** a system for arranging time into days, weeks, months, and years. **2.** a table or chart showing such an arrangement, usually for a single year.

civilization [siv′ ə lə zā′ shən] **n.** **1.** the stage in the progress of human beings when arts, sciences, government, etc., are developed. **2.** the way of life of a people, nation, or period.

conqueror [käng′ kər ər] **n.** a person who gets or gains by using force as by winning a war.

develop [di vel′ əp] **v.** **1.** to make or become larger, fuller, better, etc. **2.** to bring or come into being and work out gradually; evolve. **3.** to become known [It developed that Pat had the highest batting average.]

1. Circle any entry word below that would not be on the same dictionary page as the guide words **adamant/arduous.**

   arrive architecture advanced

2. List each entry word that has two syllables.

   ____

3. Write the entry word that rhymes with *danced.*

   ____

4. Write each entry word that has a secondary accent mark.

   ____

5. Write the entry word whose first syllable has the same vowel sound as the word *bark.*

   ____

Directions Write the number of the meaning of the word in boldface print that is used in each sentence below.

____ **1.** Ancient Egypt was a **civilization** that flourished over 5,000 years ago.

____ **2.** The Egyptians were very **advanced** in medicine and astronomy.

____ **3.** They devised a 365-day **calendar** based on the movement of the sun.

____ **4.** They **developed** picture writing into a complicated system of symbols.

____ **5.** The Great Pyramid is a well-known example of Egyptian **architecture.**

Directions Suppose you have just finished writing the report below. Proofread the paragraphs. Correct each error in spelling or in the endings added to words. Circle each error and write the correction above it. The dictionary entries on page 157 will help you.

Hint It's a good idea to proofread what you have written. Use the dictionary to check for spelling errors and to make sure that you are using words correctly.

According to modern scientists, two of the most important early Latin American civilizations were the Mayan and the Aztec. Mayan civilition was developed on the Yucatán Peninsula and the lowlands of Guatemala. Beginning around the first century and develeping rapidly, Mayan civlisation reached its peak from 200 to 800 A.D. The Mayan Indians were skilled astronomers, with an advanceed and highly accurate calendar that is still admired today. Creating remarkable art and arcitescshur the Maya were also the first Indians in America to create an advanst system of writing.

The Aztec Indians developed their civalizashun to the north of the Maya, in the Valley of Mexico. Their civilization came toward the end of the long period of development of the Central American Indains and included large cities and a well-organized government that ruled large populations. When the Spanish conkeror Cortes arriveed in Mexico in the 1500s, he found a highly advanst Aztec culture.

General Rules

Short-Vowel Rule: If a word or syllable has only one vowel and it comes at the beginning or between two consonants, the vowel is usually short–**am, is, bag, fox**.

Long-Vowel Rule I: If a syllable has two vowels, the first vowel is usually long and the second vowel is silent–**rain, kite, cane, jeep, ray**.

Long-Vowel Rule II: If a word or syllable has one vowel and it comes at the end of the word or syllable, the vowel is usually long–**we, go, pony**.

Y as a Vowel Rule:
1) If **y** is the only vowel at the end of a one-syllable word, **y** has the sound of **long i–fly, by**.
2) If **y** is the only vowel at the end of a word of more than one syllable, **y** usually has the sound of **long e–silly, baby**.

Soft C and G Rule: When **c** or **g** is followed by **e, i,** or **y,** it is usually soft–**ice, city, change, gym**.

To make a word **plural:**
1) Usually just add **s–cats, dogs, kites**.
2) If a word ends in **x, z, ss, sh,** or **ch,** usually add **es–foxes, dresses, peaches**.
3) If a word ends in **y** preceded by a consonant, change the **y** to **i** and add **es–flies, fairies, babies**.
4) If a word ends in **f** or **fe**, usually change the **f** or **fe** to **v** and add **es–wolf/wolves, knife/knives**.
5) If a word ends in **o**, usually just add **s** to make the word plural. Some words are made plural by adding **es–potato/potatoes, tomato/tomatoes, hero/heroes**.
6) Some words change their vowel sound in the plural form–**man/men, tooth/teeth, mouse/mice**.

To add other suffixes:
1) When a short-vowel word ends in a single consonant, usually double the consonant before adding a suffix that begins with a vowel–**running, hummed, batter**.
2) When a word ends in silent **e**, drop the **e** before adding a suffix that begins with a vowel–**baking, taped, latest**.
3) When a word ends in **y** preceded by a consonant, change the **y** to **i** before adding a suffix other than **ing–cried, crying, happily, funnier, ponies, trying**.

To make a noun show **possession**:
1) Add **'s** to a singular noun–**dog's, James's, child's**.
2) Add an apostrophe only to a plural noun that ends in **s–boys', the Browns', babies'**.
3) Add **'s** to a plural noun that does not end in **s–mice's, children's, women's**.

To divide words into **syllables**:
1) A one-syllable word is never divided–**day, switch**.
2) Divide a compund word between the words that make up the compound word–**in-to, sun-shine**.
3) When a word has a suffix, divide the word between the base word and the suffix–**health-ful, kind-ly**.
4) When a word has a prefix, divide the word between the prefix and the base word–**dis-please, re-place**. Some prefixes have more than one syllable–**in-ter-change, o-ver-charge**.
5) When two or more consonants come between two vowels in a word, the word is usually divided between the first two consonants–**al-most, doc-tor**.
6) When a single consonant comes between two vowels in a word, the word is usually divided after the consonant if the first vowel is short–**drag-on, rob-in**.
7) When a single consonant comes between two vowels in a word, the word is usually divided before the consonant if the first vowel is long- **pi-lot, fa-mous**.
8) When a vowel is sounded alone in a word, the vowel is a syllable in itself–**u-nit, dis-o-bey**.
9) When two vowels come together in a word and are sounded separately, divide the word between the two vowels–**gi-ant, sci-ence**.
10) When a word ends in **le** preceded by a consonant, divide the word before that consonant–**cir-cle, nee-dle**.

Definitions

The **vowels** are **a, i, u, o, e,** and sometimes **y** (when it has the sound of **long i** or **long e**) and **w** (when it is part of a vowel digraph, as in **cow**.)

The **consonants** are all the remaining letters of the alphabet and usually **y** and **w**.

A **consonant blend** consists of two or more consonants sounded together so that each consonant can be heard–**black, train, swim, spring, fast, lamp**.

A **consonant digraph** consists of two consonants that together represent one sound–**when, thin, this, church, sheep, pack, know, white**.

A **vowel digraph** is an irregular double vowel that does not follow Long-Vowel Rule I–**school, book, bread, auto, yawn, eight.**

A **diphthong** consists of two vowels blended together to form a compound speech sound–**cloud, boy, oil, cow, new**.

A **compound word** is made from two or more smaller words–**doghouse (dog house), sandbox (sand box)**.

A **contraction** is a short way to write two words as one. It is made by writing the two words together, leaving out one or more letters, and replacing the missing letters with an apostrophe (**'**).

Synonyms are words that have the same or almost the same meaning.

Antonyms are words that are opposite or almost opposite in meaning.

Homonyms are words that sound alike but have different meanings and usually different spellings.

Homographs are words that are spelled the same, but have different meanings and different word backgrounds. Some homographs have different pronunciations.

A **base word** is a word to which a prefix or suffix may be added to form a new word–**printer, unpack, likely**.

A **root** is a word part to which a prefix or suffix may be added to form a new word–**introduction, prospector, reduce**.

A **suffix** is a word part that is added at the end of a base word to change the base word's meaning or the way it is used–**sprinter, darkness, helpful**.

A **prefix** is a word part that is added at the beginning of a base word to change the base word's meaning or form a new word–**recycle, unwrap, disappear**.